Editor
Stephanie Buehler, M.P.W., M.A.

Editorial Project Manager
Ina Massler Levin, M.A.

Editor in Chief
Sharon Coan, M.S. Ed.

Illustrators
Howard Chaney

Cover Artist
Jeff Sutherland

Art Coordinator
Cheri Macoubrie Wilson

Creative Director
Elayne Roberts

Imaging
Ralph Olmedo, Jr.

Product Manager
Phil Garcia

Publishers
Rachelle Cracchiolo, M.S. Ed.
Mary Dupuy Smith, M.S. Ed.

A Word A Week

EXTRICATE
Voracious
Incognito
COSMOPOLITAN
RETROSPECT
PETRIFIED
SUBAQUEOUS
FRIVOLOUS

Author

Ruth Foster, M.A.

Teacher Created Materials, Inc.
6421 Industry Way
Westminster, CA 92683
www.teachercreated.com
ISBN-1-57690-516-0
©1999 Teacher Created Materials, Inc.
Made in U.S.A.

Teacher Created Materials

Table of Contents

The Kindergarten Connection

Think back to kindergarten and you are almost certain to recall a huge calendar tacked to a bulletin board. The name of the month, the days of the week, and numbers for dates were pinned all around. Each morning, one child was chosen to find the date and pin it to the appropriate square on the calendar grid. A discussion usually followed about the day of the week, the days that preceded and followed it, and any other special things to note, such as upcoming holidays or events. At the beginning of the year, some children may have been a little lost; perhaps they could not yet name the days of the week or had trouble with concepts such as "the day after tomorrow." But by the end of the year, nearly everyone was able to fluently talk about the calendar.

Teaching vocabulary by using *A Word A Week* is analogous to using the kindergarten calendar. A single word is introduced each day, with the dialogue and discourse surrounding the word developing students' deeper understanding of language. *A Word A Week* not only helps students to grasp the meaning of words but also to recognize word roots, to analyze new and unfamiliar words, to become more articulate, and to strengthen social skills through better communication.

A Word A Week will help students recognize that language is a code—that letters strung together produce words unique in both sound and meaning. With the focus on just one word, children are able to learn exact nuances of meaning that can be found within a given word. Words will become what they are meant to be—tools for clarity of verbal and written expression.

This book provides a link between the classroom and the world outside. Words are used in every situation that a child encounters. This book helps the child to become aware of and listen carefully to the words he or she hears. Even if a child does not remember all the words presented, the foundation has been laid for building an understanding of language and its meaning.

Choosing Words for the Program

The words contained in *A Word A Week* have been chosen quite often because they are fun or even downright silly. More importantly, the words have been chosen because they are ones that children will come across again and again in their academic and personal lives as they read and listen.

The words are also carefully sequenced so that each subsequently presented word builds upon others that preceded it. Yet, because each word is presented in a complete lesson, a teacher may commence with any word and then proceed at random, if desired. A teacher may also decide to pick out words that correspond to a particular lesson being taught during the week.

As the school year continues, the child hopefully will begin to notice times when newly acquired words apply or could be used. As the child begins to use the word in his or her own verbal and/or written communication, the child will understand that language is a manageable and useable code.

Latin Root Words

Many of the words were chosen because of their specific Latin roots. For example, most children know the meaning of and are familiar with the word *incredible*. The word *credible* is one of the words presented so that the root, *cred*, can be recognized and taught. From the root word, the words *credulous, incredulous, credit,* and *creed* are extrapolated. The prefix *in* is also discussed. In fact, several words with the *in* prefix are taught, providing continual reinforcement.

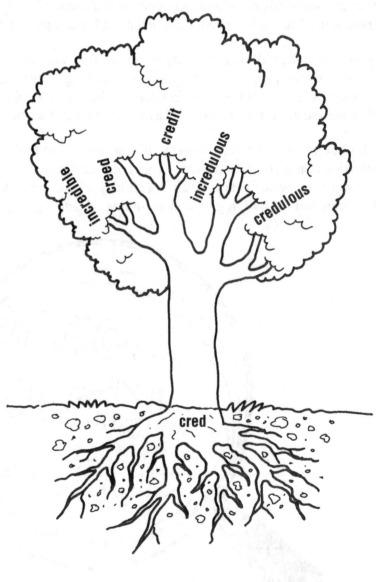

Thus, while the lesson has been on the word *credible,* the teacher has the ability, depending on his or her students' age and level, to expand in several teaching directions. A teacher may not expect students to memorize specific Latin roots, but the introduction of Latin roots allows the students to get a sense of the origins of language and its history. Language will not be seen as dead and static; language is full of change and development. The benefits of learning Latin roots will also be apparent when students study a foreign language or study for college entrance exams.

Choosing Words for the Program *(cont.)*

The Foreign Language Connection

In several places throughout *A Word A Week,* connections are made between English and foreign languages. For example, the word *malicious* contains the Latin root *mal; mal* means *bad* in Spanish. Such connections allow students to see that language is a global phenomenon and that languages are intertwined and linked with one another.

This connection can be used to develop lessons in history, government, and social studies. In addition, when the student begins to learn a foreign language, the process will not seem so intimidating. The new language will be seen as a code that has intersections with his or her own primary language.

If there is a child present in the classroom who speaks a second language, the introduction of such words presents a time when he or she can demonstrate knowledge of the primary language. These students may also find that this study of language helps them make connections to primary English speakers as they see how words unite them.

Language and Sound

Students love to play with sounds. Particular words do sound funny. Too often as adults we forget to take pleasure from the way our tongue snaps against the palette to form certain sounds. Words like *irked* and *perturbed* were included, in part, for the way they sound; they are simply enjoyable to say and hear.

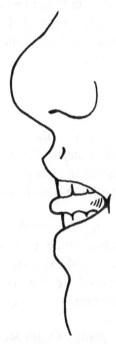

Just as a particular phrase from a television ad or a character in a movie becomes popular with children, it is hoped that some of the words in *A Word A Week* will begin to take on a particular charm for their uses. To encourage this, proper articulation and enunciation are stressed.

Words were also chosen for the positive or negative feelings evoked by their sound. Ask a child if he or she would rather be with a person who is perturbing or scintillating. Most will answer *scintillating* without even knowing its meaning; they are responding to the soft, undulating sound of the word. When asked questions like this, children seem to take delight, even if they answer incorrectly. (Take the word *upbraid,* for example, which sounds positive but definitely is not.) Exercises like these make students listen to words in a way in which they may not have done so before. Sound, then, adds a new dimension to the code.

Program Considerations

English as a Second Language

For students for whom English is a second language, *A Word A Week* vocabulary words are a valuable addition to their becoming confident, fluent speakers of English. The words being introduced are generally new to both English and non-English speaking students alike; patterns among words, particularly those with Latin roots, are stressed. Pronunciation of English language vowels sounds and accented syllables are reinforced because the words are articulated and repeated many times during a lesson.

Word Classification

Lessons on *garrulous, gullible,* and *tenacious* have questions in them that help children think about the world and objects in new ways. Are there garrulous children in the classroom? Is a particular animal tenacious? What actions would lead someone to think that another person is gullible?

Just as the concept of negative numbers opens up new dimensions in math, so, too, does teaching vocabulary. When a historical figure such as Abraham Lincoln, Dwight Eisenhower, or Martin Luther King, Jr., is mentioned, the children can begin to think of them in more multidimensional terms. Are these figures benevolent, malicious, lethargic, pedestrian, or tenacious? Or are they some combination of these adjectives? Such questions are thought-provoking and can help students articulate richer descriptions of people, things, and events.

Standardized Tests

Approximately 80 percent of the words on the Scholastic Aptitude Test (SAT) are recycled on different versions of the exam. For example, a particular word may be in an answer choice for a question on antonyms on one version, then appear in a section on reading comprehension on another version. Often the word will be altered slightly with the addition of a particular prefix or suffix.

A Word A Week prepares students for these words. Nearly every word chosen for this book has been on the SAT. In addition, the lessons help students understand how to break down unknown words. By learning and practicing word detective skills, students are ready with many of the tricks that help one become a wise test taker. Students will be able to look at a word for its familiar parts. They can then extrapolate and use context to determine meaning.

As it may be several years before many of your students actually take the SAT, using these words now will provide them with a great deal of experience. The lessons with these words reinforce in a fun, oral, and stress-free manner skills that will help them learn in many classroom and personal situations.

Program Considerations *(cont.)*

Nonreaders and *A Word A Week*

Many children—not just nonreaders—are intimidated by "big" words. They skip over them when they are reading, and they never use them in writing. Knowing roots and having practiced word analysis and deduced meaning from context, students can develop maturity in their approach to unknown words. They can be encouraged to think of themselves as word detectives who can unscramble the clues contained in a word's code, rather than seeing themselves as being powerless in the face of unknown language.

For nonreaders, learning these words in a way that breaks them down into their most basic elements can demonstrate to them that they can learn difficult vocabulary. For some nonreaders, being required to listen to the lesson can help them build their receptive and oral vocabulary, which is an essential skill. In addition, for children who participate in pull-out programs, learning these words with the entire class is an affirmation that expectations are the same for them as they are for other children. They may be below grade level in reading, but when it comes to listening and verbal communication, they can be among their peers.

We speak to young children constantly, and while doing so, we do not only use sounds that the child is able to articulate. We know that children need to listen to adults speak for many months and even years before they can speak with correct pronunciation and grammar. Why should we stop this process simply because a child reaches school age? Should entering a classroom preclude a child from hearing words he or she cannot yet read or write?

At the elementary school where *A Word A Week* was first tried, the principal told the story of a boy who was in a daily pull-out program. The boy was something of a troublemaker, and many teachers had all but given up hope of his learning. One day the boy was helping the principal move some boxes. The principal noticed that the boy was looking at the words printed on the cardboard. Suddenly the boy asked, "What does this say?" The principal told him the word. The boy repeated the word several times, then said, "This word is going to be my extra 'word a week'." It seemed that through use of this program, the boy had made the connection between the code of letters, words, and their meanings.

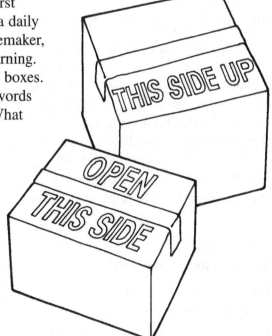

Classroom Procedures

Where to Start

A Word A Week is designed to be used in sequence, beginning with the word *garrulous*. Each word is then presented in order, as previously presented words are used in subsequent lessons. However, it is not necessary to have previously learned any of the words in order to understand a lesson. That is, lessons can be presented independently of each other, and the teacher is free to choose where to begin and the sequence of presentation. Some teachers may opt to start at the beginning and go straight through the book, teaching a word a week until the school year is up. Others may choose words according to a plan that reinforces other lessons that will be taught. In any scenario, students will learn the meaning of any word that is presented.

If an entire school is using *A Word A Week,* the teacher will want to use the same word that the rest of the school is using. Teachers will need to know in advance what these words will be. The program can be continued over several years, with teachers instructing students in new words and reinforcing words that were previously taught.

Presenting the Words

A Word A Week is designed to be read aloud by the teacher. Simply write the word on the board, overhead, or on a sentence strip and read it aloud to the students. Then read aloud the selection. Be lively and conversational in tone, as you want to capture students' interest. Feel free to improvise and add your own ideas as you read.

Number of Words to Be Taught

The simple answer to the question "How many words should I teach over the course of the school year?" is one a week. Yet this book has been written so that regardless of school calendars and holidays, a teacher has maximum flexibility to teach as many words as he or she feels the class is capable of learning. Remember, this book does not have to be finished from beginning to end in order to be useful.

Here are some ideas to consider:

- Due to holidays, early dismissal days, or weeks with heavy testing scheduled, a teacher may prefer not to present a lesson. When the normal schedule resumes, the teacher can simply resume teaching where he or she left off.

Classroom Procedures *(cont.)*

Number of Words to Be Taught *(cont.)*

- A teacher may wish to present two words a week, perhaps on Monday and Wednesday. There are enough words included in this book to do so.

- A teacher may have a particular group of children for more than one year, perhaps due to the way in which the reading program is taught in his or her school. In this case, the book provides enough words so that students are not subject to undesirable repetition.

- Some teachers may participate in cooperative programs. The first teacher can simply pass along the book, marked at the lesson where he or she left off. The second teacher then initiates lessons at that mark.

- There may be times during the week when the teacher needs a filler. A word may be presented simply for fun or to generate dialogue. The teacher may not mention this word again, but just by introducing it, he or she has demonstrated that words are interesting, fun, and worth discussing.

- A teacher may choose to pull out several words to teach prior to a particular writing assignment because they are especially appropriate or because the words were found in the reading selection assigned for that week.

Designating a Time

Just as many teachers have set times for oral language or silent reading, there should be a set time for presenting a new word. Because the words are explained in an interactive way with the teacher addressing the children and soliciting responses for which there are no right or wrong answers, *A Word A Week* provides a time when class cohesion can be initiated or rebuilt.

This type of communal activity may be very important, if not vital, in situations where children are pulled out to participate in different programs or where students are working at different levels and in separate groups. The following are some suggested times to use *A Word A Week:*

- The obvious choice is to present a new word on Monday. Mondays, however, are often crowded with new things for students to learn. Try teaching new words on Tuesday instead so that students can really focus on the skills you are trying to teach.

March

Sunday	Monday	Tuesday	Wednesday	Thursday	Friday	
	1	2 Introduce new word	3	4	5	6
7	8	9	10	11	12	1

Classroom Procedures *(cont.)*

Designating a Time *(cont.)*

- Whatever day you choose to present a new word, try to work in a review session. Ask students if they can recall the pronunciation, the root word, or any particular meaning. Can they use the word in a sentence? Depending on your interest, you may even wish to give out a raffle ticket to any student who is able to use the word during class and then have a weekly or monthly drawing for a small prize.

- Many teachers choose to present words in the morning, thus providing a maximum time for word usage throughout the day.

- Some teachers choose to present a word immediately after lunch or recess, using the lesson to rein in and refocus the children after their outdoor play.

- A new word can be presented at the beginning of a lesson in reading or writing. Encourage students to see if they can use what they have learned in that day's assignment.

- If the entire school is participating in *A Word A Week,* the word may be part of morning announcements. The age and level of one's students would determine how much time is spent reinforcing and discussing the word.

Spelling Reinforcement and Practice

Though words can be presented without any actual spelling lesson, the following practice can provide a nonthreatening review of spelling techniques. To conduct a spelling lesson, do the following:

- Write the word clearly on the board or on a sentence strip pinned to a bulletin board.

- Repeat the word often so that letters are reinforced by sound.

- Ask any number of the following questions:

  — How many letters are in this word? (Count together, if desired.) Recite all the letters out loud together.

  — How many vowels are in this word? What are they?

  — How many syllables are in this word? A good technique for breaking a word into syllables is to put one's hand under one's chin; every time the chin hits the hand, it counts as a syllable.

  — What is the first syllable? second? third?

- Write the word in the air together, reciting letters as you do so. Cover up the first letter and ask, "Which letter did I cover?" Then cover the first two letters and ask, "Which two letters did I cover?" Continue until the entire word has been spelled.

- Write the word on a piece of paper using any or all of these methods: printing, cursive, with eyes closed (children love this), or even behind one's back.

Note: *A Word A Week* words are great for earning bonus points on weekly spelling tests.

Classroom Procedures (cont.)

Dictionary Reinforcement

Many students are uncomfortable with using the dictionary because they are still uncertain of alphabetized letter sequencing. Every time a new word is introduced, use it as an opportunity to practice alphabetizing by doing the following:

- Designate a bulletin board to "A Word A Week Alphabetizing."

- As each word is introduced, it should be printed on a sentence strip or similar piece of paper. The word can then be pinned up on the bulletin board.

- As each new word is introduced, it is placed on the bulletin board alphabetically. Children can then actually see words moved around to fit in the new word. They will develop a sense of sequencing with visual reinforcement.

- To provide a more kinesthetic experience, have a student or a pair of students work together to move words around when a new word is introduced.

- Ask appropriate questions for the newly introduced word, such as the following:

   — With what letter does this word begin?

   — Where does this letter fit in the alphabet?

   — Are there any other words that start with this letter?

   — If more than one word begins with this letter, how do we know which word goes first?

- You can, of course, request that children use a dictionary or a computer program to actually look up the word. If this is done in class, ask the following questions before children begin the task:

   — Does this word start with a letter that is in the first half of the dictionary or the second?

   — If I open the dictionary to the letter **S**, for example, would I look before the letter **S** or after the letter **s** to find this word?

- Children can also be asked to look up the word at another time during the day or as homework. In this case, the following questions can be posed:

   — On what page number was the word found?

   — Was the word in the left- or right-hand column?

   — Was the word in the upper or lower half of the page?

   — What was the first, second, or third word above or below the assigned word?

   — In what third of the dictionary was the word found?

Classroom Procedures *(cont.)*

Word Usage

Students should be encouraged to use the words they have learned throughout the school day. This can be elicited by doing any of the following:

- Keep a running list of the words taught on the chalkboard or designated bulletin board. (This could be the same list used for teaching alphabetizing [page 11].)

- If the *A Word A Week* program is being utilized by the entire school, words could be placed on a special principal's bulletin board in the cafeteria or in a prominent place in the school hallway. The word could also be written on the board in the art and music classrooms.

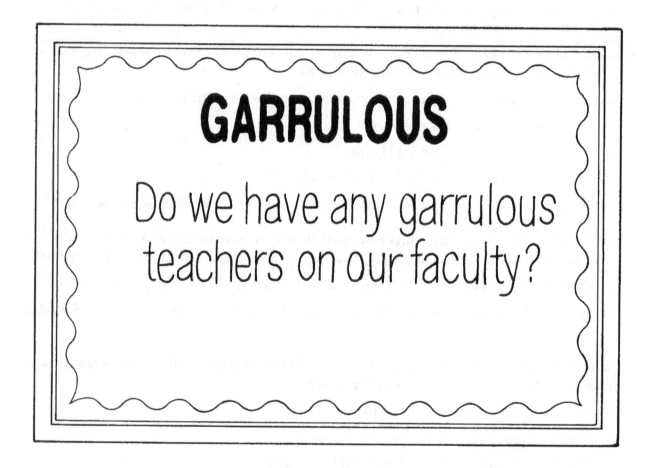

- If students have journals or personal dictionaries, the children can copy the word into their books.

- Make a tally mark every time the word is used appropriately throughout the school day on the chalkboard. This will reinforce number sense and record keeping at the same time.

- When assigning a writing topic, query the children as to whether any of the words previously studied might be appropriate to include in their compositions.

- When introducing a person, event, or thing—whether it be in a science, history, or math lesson—ask the students if any of the words studied could be used in a description.

Classroom Procedures *(cont.)*

Word Usage *(cont.)*

To encourage the use and awareness of these words outside the classroom, children can be asked to share experiences.

- Newspaper headlines can be brought in or the sentence can be copied from where students saw the word used in a book or magazine.

- A log book can be kept in a special place (perhaps by the list of the words) where children can write down where and when they heard the word in conversation, on television, or on the radio. In addition, newspaper clippings or copies of sentences could be pasted into the log book.

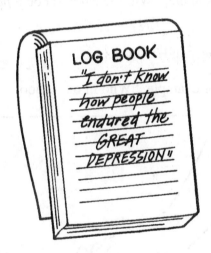

- The log book can also be used to record a situation a student witnessed where the word might apply. For example, if he or she saw something *perturbing* or *waxing and waning*, then the student can record the event, being sure to use the word in the description.

- If the teacher finds the log book too onerous for her students, she can simply ask for word anecdotes. Once the children know there will be discussions, they will start noticing and remembering the words more readily.

- A child can copy the word down onto a flash card, and the card can be taped to the refrigerator door for the week. The child can then report back if, when, and how the word was used at home.

- If the teacher has a system of weekly status reports which the parent has to sign and return, a box can be added for the parent to check if the child used the designated word at home at least once during the week.

- If the entire school is utilizing *A Word A Week,* a question about the word could be put on every weekly or monthly school bulletin.

School-Wide Implementation

A school-wide implementation of the *A Word A Week* program can help reinforce the students' learning. School administrators can be instrumental in setting the tone for an enthusiastic, cohesive environment. It is still up to each individual teacher as to how *A Word A Week* will be used in the classroom, but the participation of administrators and the knowledge that every child is learning the same new word each week can only benefit both vocabulary knowledge and school spirit.

There are more than enough words in the *A Word A Week* program that a school will never need to recycle words before students graduate. Though the easiest scenario would be to work straight through the book, it is still possible to pick out specific words that apply to immediate concerns.

A school-wide program can be implemented by doing some or all of the following:

- Tell the word for the week during morning announcements. It may not be feasible to cover the entire lesson, but just hearing the word spoken and defined starts the process of recognition. Depending on the format of school announcements, the word may simply be repeated a few times, put into a sentence, or contained within a question (for example, "Will the cafeteria be a *pacific* place today?").

- Display the word prominently in the cafeteria, school office, and hallways.

- Have a question about the word in a prominent place. For example, "Who in our school has *ardent* feelings for [insert the name of the latest celebrity heartthrob]?"

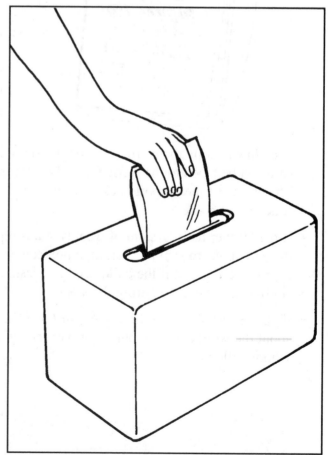

- Provide a box in the office where a child can drop in a slip of paper with his or her name on it and a sentence in which the word has been appropriately used. (Younger children can simply write the word neatly in a primary color or in cursive.) At the end of the week, an administrator pulls out a slip in a random drawing; the winner receives a free spelling point, is allowed to go to the front of the dismissal line, or receives some other reward.

- Tell students that the principal or some other designated person can stop them at any time and ask them the meaning of the word of the week. A correct answer can earn congratulations for the entire class or a point for a school-wide competition.

- Give classes the opportunity to pick the word for the week. Teachers can read aloud from a short list and let students pick by sound, meaning, or some other criteria.

A Note to Homeschoolers

Though this book is addressed primarily to school teachers, this book can also be a valuable tool for parents who have chosen to homeschool. The vocabulary words presented in these lessons can be used to augment any reading or writing program. In addition, just as the presentation of these words can be used when classroom students need to be refocused, so too can these lessons be used in the same way for one or several children of varying ages and academic levels at home.

The dictionary skills and spelling procedures are all equally applicable to the homeschooled child, and they can be adjusted to fit the immediate level and concerns of the student. For example, though a particular word may be presented to all the children, the activities that each child performs are specifically tailored for him or her. One child may simply say the word aloud to work on enunciation. Another may write the word in the air, practicing letter formation. More academically-advanced children may be asked to use it in a sentence or story or perhaps point the word out when they see or hear it being used.

This book is also an asset to a homeschooling program because the words do not have to be presented in a specific order. Which word and in what number can be determined by what the child is presently studying. The questions, riddles, and puzzles given at the end of the written discourse about a word can be either disregarded or interwoven into other lessons.

Through the use of this book, the parent is strengthening vocabulary. It reinforces the concept that language is an expressive code that can be broken apart and understood. Vocabulary is not found only in academic texts. Vocabulary is in all aspects of our lives, and acquiring vocabulary is a manageable skill.

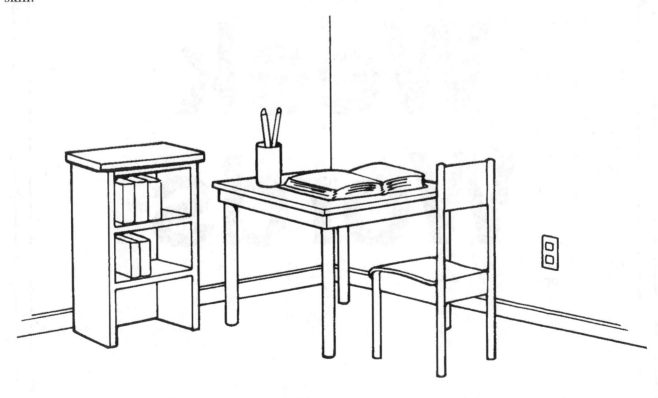

A
Word
A
Week
Words

garrulous

Garrulous! What a fun word! Everyone say it quickly five times as fast as you can. Isn't it fun the way it rolls off the tongue?

Now look around you and try to guess who is the most garrulous in the class, just from the sound of the word. Does everyone have someone in mind? Before we see if your guess came close to the meaning of the word, listen to this poem and then decide if you would pick the same person:

> *Garrulous Gerald was very social,*
> *Very verbal, and very vocal.*
> *He loved to talk to everyone—*
> *He had so much to say, he was never done.*

Garrulous is used to mean that someone talks a lot. It means that someone likes to tell stories and goes on and on and on. Were you right with your guess? Was the person you chose garrulous? Are you garrulous?

If animals could talk, would a turtle be garrulous? A hungry dog? A monkey? A lizard?

Will there be garrulous students today in the cafeteria? Is it all right to be garrulous there, as long as one is not too loud? Where else do students tend to be garrulous?

perturbed

Isn't *perturbed* a great-sounding word? Perturbed! Everyone say it along with me. Listen again to hear how *perturbed* sounds. If someone said, "I am feeling quite perturbed," do you think that person would be particularly happy?

To be perturbed means to be upset, anxious, or disturbed. If you opened up your lunch box today and found that you had a sandwich of peanut butter and mustard, you would be perturbed. If you forgot your homework, your teacher would be perturbed. And if your pet snake got loose and ended up in one of the classroom desks, the snake, you, and everyone else would be perturbed. So the next time something is bothering you, say, "I will not allow myself to be perturbed!"

Now think: Who would you find more perturbing, a little sister who tied your shoelaces together or an older brother who drank all the milk?

And here's another thought: The largest eye ever recorded was found on the Atlantic giant squid. One squid found in Canada had an eye measuring 15³/₄ inches wide. Would you find it perturbing to look up and see one of those eyes staring at you?

myriad

Myriad is a wonderful word. It's fun to say, and guess what? It is a word that goes with numbers. *Myriad* comes from an ancient Greek word meaning 10 thousand. This word is often used to mean that there are too many things to count.

If someone asked you to count the words in a dictionary, how long do you think it would take? It would take a long time because there is a myriad of words—thousands of them—in the dictionary.

Is there anyone in class who has read a myriad of books? How about everyone in the class combined?

Do you think you could say *myriad* a myriad of times? Is there a myriad of reasons why you should not be the one who takes out the garbage? Can you think of a myriad of reasons that your class should have five minutes of extra recess?

Activity: Use a chess board. Put one grain of rice on the first square. The next day, put two grains of rice on the second square. The third day, double this amount again so that there are four grains of rice. Continue to double the amount every day. How many days and squares before there is a myriad of rice?

pedestrian

You have all heard of a pedestrian crosswalk, and so you may be thinking, "*Pedestrian* is an easy word. A pedestrian is someone who walks." You would be right, but now listen to how the word *pedestrian* is used in this poem:

> *"No one should be a pedestrian thinker,"*
> *cried out our teacher, Mrs. Brinker.*
> *"Be creative, be fun, be wild—*
> *But please, don't be a boring child."*

The word *pedestrian* can mean that you don't have much of an imagination—that you are quite commonplace, ordinary, and dull and have little creativity.

Was Thomas Edison a pedestrian thinker? No! We have him to thank for the light bulb and talking movies. But the public school he attended as a boy thought Edison was pedestrian, and out of frustration, Edison's mother pulled him out of school and taught him herself at home. Genius, then, is often hidden—so before you pass judgment, remember that someone who you assume to be pedestrian may actually be very creative.

How about a woman like Harriet Tubman? Was she pedestrian? No! Thanks to her courage and free thinking, many slaves were brought safely to the North and to freedom.

Is this a pedestrian school? No! Not with extraordinary students like you! What is the most nonpedestrian thing you have ever done?

arduous

Arduous is a word that means that something is hard to do. *Arduous* suggests that a long struggle is required and that great effort is demanded. An arduous task or job is one that takes lots of hard work and is very difficult.

Climbing Mt. Everest is arduous. Some people think that playing baseball in 100° weather is arduous, while others think it is fun.

Some things are arduous at first but get easier later. For example, learning to swim may be arduous in the beginning, but it gets easier with practice and then becomes just plain fun.

If your teacher tells you to write a report with a myriad of pages, try telling him or her, "Please do not give us such an arduous task!"

Many people eat *sushi*, snacks of rice and raw fish. When it is prepared properly, it is considered to be a delicacy—something wonderful and delicious. How about you? Would you find eating sushi arduous? What about eating "desert chicken," or rattlesnake? Would you consider that to be an arduous task? What else might be arduous to eat?

impeccable

Impeccable means perfect—nothing wrong, couldn't be better, faultless. When one does everything right on a school paper, it has been done impeccably. When one is quiet when told to be by the teacher, one is behaving impeccably.

If you are being chased by a nasty dog, a dog so close on your heels that you can feel its breath, and you jump through the front door of the school the instant before it attacks you, then your timing is impeccable— you got through the door at the perfect moment.

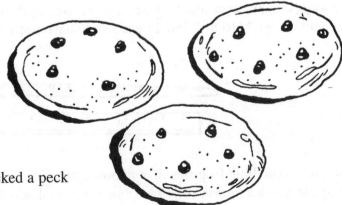

Some people think that chocolate chip cookies have an impeccable taste? What do you think tastes impeccable?

Can you say the tongue twister "Peter Piper picked a peck of pickled peppers" impeccably?

serpentine

How many of you know what a serpent is? A serpent is a snake. Now think of how snakes move. What do they do? They turn and twist and wind around and around. Now how many of you can hear the word serpent in the new word, *serpentine*? Consider what you know about serpents and try to decide what the word *serpentine* means.

Serpentine means something that has a twisting and turning form or movement. When you are playing tag and someone is chasing you, do you run in a straight line or one that is serpentine as you try to trick the person chasing you?

Soccer is a game where it is expected that players will run in a serpentine way, dodging and twisting away from other players. In baseball, though, if one ran out of the base lines, one would be out. One cannot run in a serpentine way in baseball.

Which is the most serpentine river—the Mississippi or the Nile? Why?

Serpentine can also mean that one is acting like a serpent, sly and crafty. The bad guy in a movie can be said to be serpentine. Hopefully no one serpentine goes to this school—only impeccable students here!

Do you believe that snakes and serpents are sometimes picked on unfairly?

herpetology

Now here is a defender of serpents and snakes! A *herpetologist* is one who studies reptiles and amphibians. Herpetologists know all about snakes, frogs, toads, and lizards.

Herpetology is not as difficult a word as it may sound because you are probably familiar with part of it. The ending, *ology*, means "study of." Think of the words *geology, zoology, biology,* and *paleontology.* A geologist studies the earth; a zoologist studies animals; a biologist, life forms; a paleontologist, past life forms like dinosaurs.

The longest snake ever recorded was a reticulated python found in Indonesia. The python reached the length of 32' 9½" (10 m)! Would you like to have been the herpetologist that figured out what it ate?

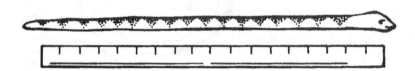

There are some little frogs that live in South America that are so poisonous that just touching one is enough to make a human ill. How could a herpetologist learn about these frogs without harming him- or herself? Do you think herpetologists ever eat frog legs?

desist

To desist means to stop, halt, cease from doing something. One should desist from picking one's nails or speaking too loudly in public, and one should definitely desist from stealing.

When is it all right to tell someone to desist? How about when someone wants to dive into the water, and no one can say how deep it is? Should we also tell someone to desist from spending all his or her money on toys? on books?

Michel Lotito of France was known as "Mr. Eat Anything." If you believe the reports, his diet included ten bicycles, a supermarket cart, seven TV sets, six chandeliers, a small airplane, and a computer. Do you think someone should have told this man to desist?

Many people desist from touching jellyfish. Would you? What happens to people who do not desist from chasing after skunks?

conundrum

Conundrum is fun to say and has a fun meaning, too. A conundrum is a riddle that is really hard to answer or a problem that is hard to solve. Research scientists are always trying to solve conundrums: how we can cure cancer, grow more food, or make our earth a clean place to live.

Do you sometimes get the feeling that math problems are conundrums? Of course, they are not. With time and practice, they are solvable; they just seem like conundrums until that time.

Who knows the answer to this conundrum: What has a bed but never sleeps, a mouth but never eats, and runs but never walks. The answer? A river.

Now here's a conundrum: You enter a locked classroom and find your coat hanging from the ceiling. The ceiling is over 12' high, and no one can reach it without help. There are no ladders, chairs, or tables in the room. All you find are your coat—and a single student standing in a pool of water. How did your coat get on the ceiling? Answer: The student stood on a huge block of ice to get it there.

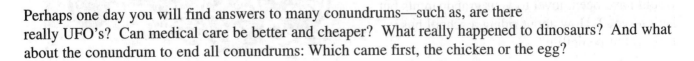

Perhaps one day you will find answers to many conundrums—such as, are there really UFO's? Can medical care be better and cheaper? What really happened to dinosaurs? And what about the conundrum to end all conundrums: Which came first, the chicken or the egg?

ludicrous

Isn't *ludicrous* a funny sounding word? The silly sound of *ludicrous* actually helps one to remember its meaning. *Ludicrous* means ridiculous. Ludicrous things are laughable and silly.

The next time someone does something really silly, such as wearing a shirt backwards or eating soup with a fork, you might just say, "You are ludicrous."

What do you think is ludicrous? Is coming home and finding an elephant in your bathtub ludicrous? Is having blue spaghetti ludicrous? How about people who wear their sunglasses indoors or on top of their heads?

Listen to this rhyme and see how many countries you can name where this poem would not apply.

> *"How ludicrous," cried Jonathon Jay,*
> *"To think that it should snow in May."*
> *Ridiculous and silly as it might be,*
> *The snow is there for all to see.*

Greenland, Iceland, Antarctica, and Canada are all places where snow is seen in May. Snow has even been recorded in Montana in May. It seems that snow in May is not all that ludicrous!

Quick, all of you! Make a ludicrous face! Now that's really silly.

novel

You are all thinking, "We know what *novel* means. A novel is a book. It is a made-up story. *Charlotte's Web* is a novel." But English is a tricky language. Many words can be used more than one way (like *pedestrian*), and *novel* is one of them.

Something that is novel is new. A novel thing is unfamiliar, not known before, of a new nature or kind. Learning how to multiply is novel at first, and then it becomes "old hat," or familiar and easy.

It was once believed that the world was flat, and that if one sailed toward the horizon, one would fall off the edge. Scientists began to question this and began to think about the world in a novel way. They felt the world was round, and they proved to be correct.

Computers are still novel. Every day they get fancier and new things are added on to them. Cars aren't novel to us anymore, but to your great grandparents they were novelties, brand new inventions called "horseless carriages." Can you think of anything else that would have been novel to your grandparents but isn't to you? How about riding a school bus? How about penicillin?

stymie

Stymie! Just from its sound, do you think you would like to be stymied?

Stymie means to block, to frustrate, to make it difficult for something to be done. If one is stymied, one is stuck, unable to go on. If one is unable to organize a report, one is stymied. The next time your teacher asks you a question and you don't know the answer, don't answer, "I don't know"—instead say, "I'm stymied."

If you were being charged by a rhinoceros, and you were running as fast as you could in a straight line—not a serpentine one—and you came to a large cliff and found that you couldn't go any further, would you feel stymied?

Cats are stymied all the time. They climb up trees, but they can't get down. Would you feel stymied if there was a big ice storm and no one had water or electricity for days and days?

When have you been stymied? Have you been stymied trying to climb a tree? beating a team? playing chess with your brother?

And perhaps you will be stymied by this riddle: What happens when someone throws a blue hat into the Red Sea? Answer: It gets wet. Would this one stymie you: When is a cook mean? Answer: When the cook beats the eggs.

colossal

Colossal means really big, enormous, huge, gigantic.

How many of you have ever ridden a roller coaster? One of the biggest roller coasters in the world is called "The Colossal." "The Colossal" is a huge, go-upside-down-and-backwards, get-sick-to-your-stomach type of roller coaster.

How many of you have ever heard of a coliseum? A coliseum is a huge place where people can go to watch games or other events. Notice how *colossal* and *coliseum* sound almost the same.

Who wants a colossal pizza for lunch with a colossal cola chaser? How about a colossal piece of cake? To celebrate the 100th birthday of the state of Alabama, a colossal cake was made that weighed 128,238 pounds!

What is the most colossal animal alive today? It is the blue whale. One blue whale was measured at a little over 102'!

How would you feel if you were the speaker in this poem?

> *I was on the savannah, down in the grass,*
> *Watching the animals slowly pass.*
> *A colossal shadow fell over my place—*
> *I quickly got up to give an elephant space!*

What would you do if a colossal shadow came over you?

extrovert

Do you think an extrovert is someone who likes to be around people and is not afraid to speak up, or do you think an extrovert would rather be alone and stay apart from others?

Here is a hint: *Ex* means "out of." If *ex* means out of, and we are talking about an extrovert, then you were right if you guessed that an extrovert is the one who is friendly and likes to be out with people. You were not being pedestrian in your thinking!

Is there anything in the word *extrovert* that reminds you of *exit*? There should be! You go out of an exit, and an extrovert loves to "go out" and be with people. Now that you know what kind of person an extrovert is, what kind of person do you think is an introvert? Does your class have more extroverts, introverts, or people in the middle? "People in the middle" are known as ambiverts, and *ambi* means *both*. An ambivert is someone who likes to be out with people and likes to be alone equally.

Who is likely to be more garrulous: an extrovert or an introvert? Does an extrovert have to be garrulous?

Do you think the way one acts depends on where one is? Could one be an extrovert at home, but be shy or introverted at school? What do you think?

plethora

Try to guess the meaning of the word *plethora* from this poem:

> *Went on a picnic, but oh dear!*
> *A plethora of pests came near.*
> *There were ants in our pants,*
> *And bugs in our mugs.*
> *Snakes in our cakes,*
> *And mice in our rice.*
> *So many, many pests, you see,*
> *That we could not rest to drink our tea.*

Plethora means "a lot"—like a huge, great, colossal amount, like too much fullness! At Thanksgiving there is a plethora of food. Some kids think that there is never a plethora of desserts, only a plethora of vegetables. What do you think?

Do any of you see the resemblance *plethora* has to the word *plenty*? If you are in the ocean, and everywhere you swim you see jellyfish, you might think, "I don't know if I want to swim in a plethora of jellyfish! Too many jellyfish for me!"

Is it good to have a plethora of homework or recesses, or is it better to have a reasonable amount of both?

gregarious

A gregarious person is one who loves company. A gregarious person loves to be social and companionable. Gregarious people are extroverts. A gregarious person would rather eat lunch with lots of people rather than eat alone. Gregarious people like group projects. They like doing things with lots of people.

In your class, there will be some people who are more gregarious than others. The opposite of being a gregarious person is being a solitary one. The world needs both types of people. What type are you? Are you gregarious, solitary, or a little of both?

Would a gregarious or a solitary person talk on the phone more? Killer whales live and hunt in groups. Are they gregarious? What about cats? Are they gregarious or solitary? Can you think of some other gregarious animals? Why do you think it is better for some animals to be gregarious?

ambidextrous

All right handers, raise your hands! Now all left handers! Usually there are more right handers. Did your class fit the bill?

But what if you could use both your left and right hand equally well? There are people who can, and they are called *ambidextrous*. There are ambidextrous batters—they bat left and right handed.

If your teacher were ambidextrous, he or she could stand in the middle of the board and write on one side with his or her left hand and then just switch the chalk to his or her right hand! Everyone would be able to see the board, no matter where they sat!

Think what one could do if he or she were ambidextrous! Would it be easier to be a carpenter? Whenever one hand got tired of nailing, you could switch to the other. What about the man described below?

> *Ambidextrous Andy could use both hands,*
> *And with them played in many bands.*
> *Sax and flute and even the drums,*
> *Hitting them evenly with both thumbs.*

Here's a conundrum you nonpedestrian students can solve: an extrovert goes out, an introvert stays in, so what does an ambivert do? (Remember that an ambidextrous person can use both hands!)

An ambivert is both an extrovert and an introvert. An ambivert would be comfortable being both gregarious and solitary.

irk

All right, impeccable students! Who remembers the word *perturbed*? Our new word, *irk*, is very closely related. *Perturbed* means that one is upset and bothered, and *irked* means that one is annoyed, bothered, and irritated.

It would be irksome to discover that you had forgotten what *perturbed* means. What irks you? What do you find irksome? Would you be irked if you looked in the refrigerator and there were only onions to eat?

Students who yell in the cafeteria are irksome. Would you be irked if someone dropped a spider down your shirt?

If you went to the cafeteria today and found out that the dessert was worms, would you be irked? In this poem, do you think Mother Cara has the right to be irked, or is she just overreacting?

> *"How irksome," Mother Cara said,*
> *"That you never, ever made your bed.*
> *I am bothered, and this is why—*
> *Listen carefully, I will not lie!*
> *There is something in-between the sheets,*
> *Hiding there to tickle your feet!"*

placid

When something is placid, it is calm and undisturbed. A placid scene is a peaceful one, one where there is tranquillity and quiet.

Have you ever held a baby? Some babies are more placid than others. Placid babies are easier to hold because they are calmer and don't get upset. Some young offspring aren't placid, especially animals like goats or pigs that squeal and move around a great deal.

Some animals are known for being more placid than others. Cows are known as being gentle and placid while grizzly bears are known for their aggressiveness and for not being placid. What do you think would happen if a placid cow sat on an angry bee?

Would sailors prefer a placid ocean or one with wild waves?

Word detectives, here is a new case, though it should not be too arduous for you to solve. The root *plac* means "please." When something is placid, it is calm and peaceful; a placid person is pleased. So if one placates a child having a temper tantrum, what has one done? The answer is that you have calmed the child; you have pleased the child and made him or her peaceful. Do you see how close the words *placid* and *placate* are?

How are you placated when you are upset or something unfair happens to you?

inclement

Stow the sails and batten down the hatches! Put on those jackets and find your hats! We're about to have inclement weather! And inclement weather is cold, wet, and stormy. If you listen to weather reports, reporters often warn about inclement conditions. Tornadoes, hurricanes, and blizzards are all part of inclement weather.

The prefix *in* means "not," and the word *clemency* means "calm or merciful." When a judge gives one clemency, the judge is a forgiving one. Clementine was a common girl's name for a while, and it meant that one was kind and full of mercy. But when you put *in* and *clement* together—wow! We get a word that means anything but mild or calm!

Inclement environments are not necessarily wet and cold; they can also be very hot and dry, like in Libya in 1992, when the highest temperature ever in the shade was reported—136° F (58° C)!

The word *inclement* might also be used to describe a place; shark-infested waters are often described as inclement.

Different parts of the world have more inclement weather than others. How would you rank where you live?

claustrophobia

When someone is claustrophobic, he or she is afraid of closed-in spaces. He or she needs room and windows. Claustrophobic people can't stand lots of people around them; they don't like the feeling of being hemmed in. Many claustrophobic people won't ride in elevators because these are small spaces, and small spaces makes such people feel trapped.

Say *claustrophobia*. Claustrophobia. Do you hear the last part, *phobia? Phobia* means "to have a fear that is so intense, so strong, it is abnormal." People have phobias about many things: dogs, spiders, and snakes—even sleeping in the dark.

Was there ever a time when you felt claustrophobic? Where would you feel the most claustrophobia—in an airplane or at the edge of the Grand Canyon? (Some people have a different sensation altogether when they stand on the edge of a high place; it's known as *vertigo*. Vertigo is a sensation of falling even though one is standing in place.) Would a claustrophobic person prefer a house with lots of windows or a house with few windows?

Here are the Latin names for a few different phobias:

acrophobia—fear of heights   arachnophobia—fear of spiders
nyctophobia—fear of the dark   musophobia—fear of mice
xenophobia—fear of strangers   emetophobia—fear of vomiting
zoophobia—fear of animals   poinophobia—fear of punishment
agoraphobia—fear of being in open or
             public places

tenacious

Tenacious can be a difficult word to learn at first but if one thinks of an octopus, the meaning of tenacious becomes much easier to remember. Think, what does an octopus have eight of? Eight tentacles! And what do those tentacles do? They hold on and never let go! They grab and stick—just like a tenacious person. *Ten* means "to hold," and many words that contain the root *ten* have something to do with sticking power and being tough and unbreakable. Being *tenacious* means that one sticks to things, that one holds on and does not give up.

Math facts are mastered with tenacity. Soccer games are won and marathons run with tenacity. Someone who is tenacious never gives up and keeps on trying. The little blue engine that said, "I think I can! I think I can! I think I can!" was tenacious.

Snapping turtles are known for being so tenacious that they never let go of what they bite. Polar bears are tenacious hunters. They cover their noses (the only part of them that is not white) with their paws and then tenaciously wait and wait and wait for seals. Can you think of other animals that are tenacious? What makes them so?

benevolent

The important thing to remember about the word *benevolent* is that *bene* means good. Lots of words have the root *bene,* and if one remembers *good*, then one has already figured out most of what the words means. With tenacity, one will remember that *bene* means good!

A benevolent person is a good and kind person. Benevolent people help others, give to charity, and are kind. A benevolent action might be giving up your seat to an elderly person or a pregnant woman.

Have you ever heard of a benefit garage sale or a benefit dance? People are raising money for the benefit, or for the good, of someone else or for a particular cause. People who organize the event or who contribute are being benevolent.

Many people today are afraid that we are forgetting how to be a benevolent society—people steal from each other, children go hungry, and we make fun of each other because of our differences. A benevolent society starts with us and is based on how we treat our classmates and each other.

There is a saying that goes, "Perform senseless acts of beauty and random kindness." Do you think that doing this would help promote benevolence? What benevolent thing could you do today?

malicious

Many of our words are related to words in other languages. *Malicious* is one of them. The word for bad in Spanish is *mal*. Someone who is malicious is bad; he or she does not act benevolently or with good intentions.

A malicious act would be one that purposely tried to ruin or hurt someone or something. If someone purposely stole someone's homework on the day it was due or ruined someone's big science project, he or she would be acting with malice.

We can see *mal* added to many other words as a prefix. Can you figure out the meanings of these words: *malnourished, malformed, maladjusted,* and *maltreated*?

Though we often think of sharks as malicious, there are some sharks, like nurse sharks, that would never attack a person. Great white sharks, on the other hand, are known to be quite malicious. We might even consider the way sharks court each other as malicious. Instead of bringing flowers, the males bite the females on the tail! Luckily, the skin on the females is very thick and seems to heal quickly.

Gossip is usually malicious. Sometimes in our effort to make ourselves feel bigger, we are malicious or mean to other people by gossiping about them. Which do you think is better to spread, maliciousness or benevolence?

amicable

Try to get an idea about the meaning of the word *amicable* from this poem:

> *Jake was amicable night and day,*
> *And with his friends he would kindly play.*
> *If he climbed a tree to look in a nest,*
> *He always let the birdies rest.*

If one is amicable, one is friendly and peaceable. Amicable neighbors do not fight over barking dogs or destroy each other's property. In a friendly way, amicable neighbors decide together what to do about any problems that come up. Amicable people are not malicious.

With so many people driving fast in cars on busy roads these days, it is best to be amicable to other drivers rather than be malicious.

Dolphins are known to be amicable animals. There have been cases where they have helped injured or exhausted swimmers to shore.

Some people feel that if two children cannot be amicable to each other, they should be made to stay together until they learn to get along. Do you agree with this?

petrified

Based on the sound of this word, who in this class would like to be petrified? Does it sound like a good thing to be?

To petrify something is to change it into stone. Who has heard of petrified wood? Petrified wood is wood that has fossilized and changed to stone.

Petrified also means that one becomes still or rigid, unable to move, as if one were a stone. One becomes petrified when one is horribly afraid or in awe of something. Watching scary movies can petrify many people. They get so petrified that they cannot get out of their seats. They are petrified with fear.

Claustrophobics are petrified by closed-in spaces. Leeches, those tenacious blood suckers, petrify many people, and so people are afraid to touch them. In some ways, this is a good thing because one should not pull leeches off of his or her skin. It is better to let them take their fill of your blood and then have them drop off. This way there is less risk of infection setting in.

What helps you to be brave and to not become petrified? Singing? Thinking of happy things?

superfluous

Is *superfluous* related to Superman? Yes, because both of them have the root *super*. *Super* means over and above, much better than ordinary. When one does something well, one has done a super job—over and above what is usual or expected.

Though the *super* in *superfluous* and *superman* mean the same thing, the words are very different. Superman is supposed to be better than ordinary people, but if something is superfluous, it is extra, more than what is needed; *superfluous* means unwanted excess.

Do you sometimes think that you are assigned a superfluous amount of homework? Superfluous actions are actions that are not needed. Perhaps someone jumps into the pool to save you and you do not need saving—you are just swimming along the bottom. Perhaps your parents yell at you to take out the garbage but you have already done it. Their words are superfluous; they are not needed. Sometimes all one wants is a "yes" or "no" answer, but the person is quite garrulous and goes on and on and on. The extra words are superfluous.

If you saw a man who was wearing three sweaters and two coats, and it was only 55° outside, you could say the man's clothing was superfluous; it was not needed.

What is superfluous about this sentence: Like, I am, like, learning, like, all these new words, like, and like, this last word we had to learn, like, it was really, like, useless.

interminable

If something is interminable, it goes on forever and ever and ever and ever. . . . Did you think I would say "ever" interminably?

If something is interminable, it never stops. *Interminable* is a great word for word detectives. Do you recognize the *in* from *inclement*? *In* means not, and so if something is interminable, it is not terminable. *Term* means "end," and so if one terminates something, one is ending or stopping it. (Can you hear the root word in *airport terminal*? The terminal is where the flights end.) If something is interminable, it cannot be stopped or it is never ending.

Have you ever had to wait for a shot at the doctor's office? Didn't the wait seem interminable, as if it were never going to end? Have you ever had to listen to a boring speech or watch a boring movie that seems to go on forever and ever? They seem interminable.

Young children often ask an interminable number of questions like the following: Why do we have noses? Why is your hair black? Why do we breathe? Why are you not a mouse? Why isn't your name Australia? Where is Australia?

Can you think of five things that you find interminable?

gullible

Gullible, gullible, gullible. Say that word as fast as you can five times. Does it sound like a serious person would be gullible? Would you like to be gullible? Hopefully, you don't! When one is gullible, one is easily tricked and deceived. One is willing to believe anything. If you said to someone, "A penny is worth more than a dime because the penny is larger than the dime," only a gullible person would believe you.

If someone offers to sell you a bridge for fifty dollars, I hope that you tell them, "Do you really think that I am that gullible?"

Only a gullible person would believe that one shouldn't tell a secret in a cornfield because there are too many ears, and only gullible people would think that a pound of rocks was heavier than a pound of feathers.

Can you think of a time when you were gullible? How about on April Fool's Day? By the way, doesn't gullible have a unique spelling with three "l's" in it? Oh! How many of you remembered that school is letting out early all this week?

vivacious

Doesn't *vivacious* sound like a better thing to be than *gullible*? Vivacious people are happy and bubbly. They are lively and fun to be with. If one is full of life, one is vivacious.

Lots of gregarious people are vivacious, but one doesn't have to be gregarious to be vivacious. An example is an ant or a honey bee. Both animals are gregarious, but they aren't exactly what one would call vivacious. Ants are single-minded when it comes to bringing food back to their colony, and honey bees are pretty serious when it comes to getting their pollen. If bees feel threatened or in danger, watch out—they are not very vivacious when they are angry!

If one were a clown, do you think one would be better at one's job if one were vivacious or solemn? How about if one were president? a movie actor or actress? a teacher? Have you ever been to a game where the crowd is especially vivacious?

The Latin word for life is *vita,* and many of our words that have *viv* or *vita* in them have to do with life. Guess what the Spanish word for life is? *Viva*! And remember that vitamins (hear the root *vita*?) are necessary for life.

Can you solve this conundrum: Which is more vivacious— the giant sloth or the tortoise?

Look up *vivacious* in the dictionary and count how many words around it have the *viv* root in them and also have a meaning that concerns life.

lethargic

Lethargic means slow. Can you say *lethargic* lethargically? Can you say *lethargic* with no energy at all? Can you say *lethargic* as slowly as you are able, without any hint of vivaciousness? *Lethargic* means without any energy at all, so we are talking really slow here.

Think about the way you feel on days when it is over 100° and the humidity (the amount of moisture in the air) is so high that it makes the air thick—so thick it feels as if you are walking through mayonnaise? You probably feel very lethargic, don't you?

If we don't get enough sleep, we often feel so lethargic, its as if we have no energy at all. Boredom makes some people lethargic, while other people become jumpy and distracted. When we are ill, we feel lethargic; we do not want to move.

Do you think that if you jumped 358 times with a jump rope while on a tightrope, like Julian Albulet in 1990, that afterwards you might feel lethargic?

pacific

Which side of the United States is the Pacific Ocean on? Is it on the east coast, bordering New York and Georgia, or on the west coast, bordering California and Oregon? Yes, the Pacific Ocean is on the west coast.

The Pacific Ocean was so-named because it was (or seemed to be) so peaceful, quiet, and tranquil. *Pacific* means calm and peaceful. Knowing that pacific means peaceful, what do you think one is doing when pacifying someone? When one pacifies someone, one is making that person more calm, more peaceful. One uses a pacifier to calm down a crying baby, for example.

If an angry orangutan came into the building and started jumping up and down in the halls, it might be pacified with a tasty banana or another tempting fruit.

Pacifists do not believe in fighting. They remain calm and peaceful. Martin Luther King, Jr., and Mohandas Gandhi were two famous pacifists. Can you find on the map what countries they came from? (Find the United States and India.)

How would you pacify a hippopotamus, with its 24" cm lips, if you found one in the locker room?

Which would you find more pacific: reading a book while sitting on a white sand beach, or watching a movie with your friends and an endless supply of popcorn?

intrepid

Intrepid. Now this word sounds like no-nonsense. Intrepid. Nothing mushy or soft here. *Intrepid* means fearless and brave, and so its meaning does seem to fit its sound. An intrepid person would be one who has no fear and is very brave. Reinhold Messner intrepidly climbed Mt. Everest by himself, without bottled oxygen. He is the only person in the world who has ever done this. It was an intrepid act.

Annie Taylor went over Niagara Falls in a barrel in 1901. Though it may have been an intrepid act to go over the falls in a barrel, many people thought that it was a foolish thing to do. Annie was lucky to survive.

One might feel *trepidation*, or fear and nervousness, when standing on the high dive, but after a few jumps, one usually begins to feel less trepidation and becomes intrepid. (Remember that *in* means "not.")

Firefighters are often intrepid, fearlessly going into burning buildings to save people. Parachutists seem intrepid. Do you think such individuals felt trepidation on their first jump?

Would you feel intrepidation or trepidation if you were on a boat that was filling with water?

fraternity

A *fraternity* is a group of people who have a common interest. A fraternity is like a club. *Frat* is Latin for brother, and a fraternity is a brotherhood. Fraternities can be formed for either social or professional reasons. Surgeons are part of the medical fraternity. If you act fraternally toward someone, you are acting like a brother to him. If you fraternize with someone, you are being friendly to him or her. Have you ever heard the saying, "Don't fraternize with the enemy"?

Here is another question: Is it wise to fraternize with a tiger? In India, a man once gave a tiger he had raised from a cub to a zoo. He became ill and could not visit his tiger for six months. When he finally went to visit his tiger, he found the animal growling and pacing inside its cage. The man intrepidly stepped over the fence and reached into the cage. "Come here," he commanded. He scratched the tiger behind its ears and under its chin. The zoo keepers stared in disbelief. It was then that they told the man that his tiger had died three months before. The tiger the man was scratching was a new tiger, so wild that all the zoo keepers were afraid of it. Do you think that man ever fraternized with tigers again?

Your goal for today: Be fraternal toward someone.

monotone

What tone of voice do you think someone uses when they speak in a *monotone*? Do you think their voice goes up and down and has lots of expression or do you think their voice is flat and level and never changes? Think about this before you answer: *mono* means one.

When someone speaks in a monotone, he or she always uses the same tone or voice. Boring! Can you imagine what it would be like to have to hear someone speak in a monotone all the time? If someone were reading aloud to you and spoke in a monotone, it would seem interminable.

Mono is part of the word monopoly. If someone has a monopoly, one person has everything. And a monocle is an eyeglass for only one eye. If something is monotonous, it seems as if it is all the same, or repetitious.

Think about how important it is not to speak in a monotone. Can you imagine going to a movie where everyone spoke in a monotone, with no one sounding excited, happy, or sad. What if your music teacher sang songs in a monotone? Take the sentence, "We're having pancakes and bacon for breakfast." Try saying it in a monotone. Now say it with excitement, and then say it as a question. What power we have in our voices when we are expressive!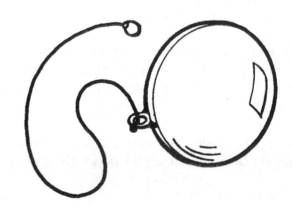

obdurate

Can you figure out what *obdurate* means in this poem:

> *Obdurate Ollie dug his heels in the sand,*
> *Refusing to go along with the plan.*
> *And so stubborn Ollie was left behind,*
> *Until he decided to change his mind.*

Obdurate means stubborn. Obdurate people do not easily change their minds. The prefix *ob* means against, so many of the words that start with *ob* end up being negative words (think of *obnoxious* and *obstacle*). When one is obdurate, one is very stubborn to the point of being obnoxious. Even the word *obdurate* sounds stubborn.

Mules are animals known for being obdurate. We often think of being very stubborn or obdurate as a bad thing, such as when we are obdurate about trying new foods, going to school, reading new books, or learning new things. But what if someone was trying to tell you to steal something, and you obdurately refused to do so?

Should one be obdurate when it comes to eating liver? How about riding a bike without a helmet?

audible

Say *audible* softly five times, as fast as you can! Were you able to say it audibly? If something is audible, it can be heard. People can hear it.

Are some of the voices in this class more audible than others? Isn't it horrible to go to a movie when the sound is inaudible? (Remember that *in* means "not," and so if something is inaudible, it cannot be heard.)

Any word that has the root *audi* in it usually has to do with sound. Can you hear and see the root *audi* in *auditorium*? We go to an auditorium to hear music or speeches. The audience listens to the sounds.

An audiologist (remember that an *ologist* means someone who studies something) studies sound. It is an audiologist who gives hearing tests and decides if people might benefit from hearing aids.

There is a new field of science, audiobiology. Can you figure out the meaning? An audiobiologist studies the sounds of animals. For example, there is one audiobiologist who is studying elephant communication. Elephants have such greatly developed audio powers (think of the size of their ears!) that they can hear and make many sounds that are inaudible to us. An audiobiologist records those sounds with very special equipment and then listens to these sounds on machines that make the sounds audible to us. What other animals do you think communicate with sounds that are inaudible to us?

bibliophile

If you heard or read this nursery rhyme as a small child, do you think you would already know what the word *bibliophile* means?

> *Sarah was a bibliophile,*
> *Loved her books and read all the while.*
> *Went to the library every day,*
> *And when offered a book, never said, "Nay."*
> *She loved their smell and feel and words,*
> *And to those who didn't read, she said, "How absurd!*
> *For books are for me a lasting joy,*
> *And are good and better than any toy."*

A bibliophile is a lover of books. If given a choice between collecting a bean bag animal or a book, a bibliophile would choose the book. *Biblio* means "book." The bibliography at the end of a report or a book is the listing of all the books that were used when writing the report or the book.

Bibliophile also contains the root word *phil*. *Phil* means "love," and thus Philadelphia is the city of love. An anglophile loves all things English, and a francophile loves all things French. An audiophile loves sounds.

Make up a list of your own *phile* words. For example, are you a chocophile (lover of chocolate) or a ratophile (lover of rats)?

trudge

Go by sound when trying to remember the meaning of this word! Trudge, trudge, trudge. Do you think *trudge* sounds like something a sad or a happy person would do? *Trudge* (sort of reminds one of sludge) is a boring, tired, sounding word, and its definition fits the way it sounds.

To trudge is to walk or march in a tired or weary way. When one trudges, one is not happy or enthusiastic. *Trudging* means that one is dragging their feet and showing no excitement.

Have you ever played so hard that, after the game, all you can do is trudge off the field to the water jug? Are you more likely to trudge when you are taking out the garbage or going to play in the sprinkler? Do you trudge after your parents when they go from store to store to store?

If you go for a 10-mile hike, on the last mile, are you running or trudging along? In a race, would your trudge change to a more lively run if you could finally see the finish line or if someone was coming up close behind you?

dehydrated

When one is dehydrated, one does not have enough water in his or her body. To hydrate means "to give water"; *hydro* means "water" and *de* means "to remove," so *dehydrate* means "to lose water."

It is very important to keep enough liquids in our bodies, as we are mostly liquid, and if we don't get enough liquids, we become sick and eventually die. That is why runners and other athletes are always drinking liquids. When we sweat, we have to replace the lost liquid by drinking extra fluids.

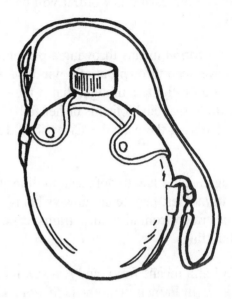

One wouldn't think of mountain climbers in the snow becoming dehydrated, but they quite often do and have to be very careful to watch for its signs. They need to drink lots of melted snow.

Raisins are dehydrated grapes. Dehydrated ice cream was invented for astronauts, and many hikers eat other types of dehydrated foods. The water was taken out of the food, and the food is rehydrated by adding water.

If you know that *hydro* means water, can you figure out what *hydrology* means? Remember that *ology* means "the study of." Hydrology is the study of water. What is hydropower? Hydrophobia? (Remember that *phobia* is "the fear of.") All of these words are built with the root *hydro*. Every time you take a drink from the drinking fountain today, think, "I won't get dehydrated today!" or "I need to hydrate myself!"

credible

Credible may be a word you are unfamiliar with, but how about *incredible*? If you find something incredible, it is not believable. If something is credible, it is believable.

Something credible also means that it is trustworthy; we have belief in it. We have credit cards because we are being trusted to pay based on our credibility, with the promise that we will pay money to the lender.

Years ago, people did not find the idea of the earth being round as credible. They found it incredible. They were incredulous that anyone would believe something so silly.

Sometimes we are too credulous, willing to believe anything. A credulous person would be one who believes that mermaids exist or that straw can be turned into gold. An incredulous person would not believe it.

With your detective skills, can you figure out what the root *cred* means? *Cred* means "belief." A creed is someone's belief. Who would you find more credible: a judge or a thief? a used car salesperson or a medical doctor? a five year old or a fifty year old? Why? Is this always true?

defenestration

Defenestration may be one of the oddest words you will ever learn. Defenestration. Unless you know Latin or French, there is little to help you figure out what defenestration means. Take a few guesses, but once you learn this word, it will be hard to forget because it has such an unusual meaning. Are you ready?

Defenestration means throwing a person or a thing out of a window. If you have been defenestrated, you have been thrown out of a window. Firefighters, though, actually practice defenestration. It is the goal of a firefighters though, that if they do defenestrate someone, that person lands on a net or on something that cushions his or her fall! Pediatricians warn against the risks of young children defenestrating themselves. Cribs should not be placed next to windows, and screens should be bolted in.

It is against the law to defenestrate litter from a car. In movies, people are always being defenestrated from airplanes, trains, cars, or tall buildings.

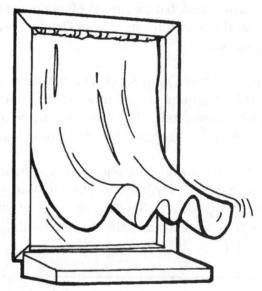

De in Latin means from, and *fenestra* means window. In French, window is *fenetre*. Can you hear these roots in defenestration?

Defenestration is a not a commonly used word (as a matter of fact, in some abridged dictionaries it is not listed at all), but it is a word that is used and known among many professionals. Our language is filled with all kinds of words!

articulate

Say *articulate* very clearly and you are already halfway to learning all about this word. To articulate something is to say it clearly and distinctly. When something is articulated, it is understood and intelligible.

Think what might happen if you were inarticulate, and the nurse asked, "Who is getting this shot?" He or she might think that you are mumbling, "Oh the shot is for me," when you really might be saying, "The shot is for my sister, Bea." What if the cook asked, "Would you like some squid with horseradish and undercooked yellow squash?" and because you were inarticulate, the cook thought you said, "As much as I can have, please," when what you really said was, "I'd rather eat limburger cheese." Remember that the prefix *in* means not; *inarticulate* means something is not spoken clearly.

Is it easier to take a spelling test when your teacher articulates each syllable clearly than when your teacher inarticulately mumbles all the words together? Would an articulate or an inarticulate person have a better chance at getting a job?

discordant

Screams, scrapes, bangs, clangs, harsh, and very unpleasant sounds are all discordant. Discordant sounds are not flowing or sweet sounds. Discordant sounds make people cover their ears and wish for quiet.

Have you every heard two cats fight? How about high-pitched shrieks on an upside down roller coaster, combined with the sound of all the other screaming riders all over the park?

Now, if there is discord, there is a lack of harmony, or getting along together. Discord can happen not only in music. People can become discordant when they do not agree. They can argue and yell at each other. Great discord can occur when states or counties are fighting over water rights. Baseball games can often become discordant, with each side screaming at the other. There was great discord in the United States during the Civil War when some states wanted to leave the United States and become a different country.

Different sounds are more discordant to some people than to others. For example, nails across a chalkboard can be so discordant to some people that they think they are going mad, while other people do not even look up from the book they are reading! You may have a special musical group or band that you like. Do adults think that the music you like is discordant?

mellifluous

Mellifluous. Mellifluous. Sounds a little more "flowy," and a lot less discordant than *discordant*! *Mellifluous* sounds like the feeling one should have if he or she is on an air mattress, cold drink in hand, gently flowing down the stream.

Think of *melody* and *melodious* (pleasing to the ear), and think of those refreshing fluids! *Mellifluous* means sweetly flowing.

There can be mellifluous thoughts: I love you; your love is like a rose; there is chocolate chip cookie dough ice cream for dessert; there is only one more long-division math problem left.

There can be mellifluous music—songs we grew up with or particular piano pieces we enjoy. There can be mellifluous sounds in nature: crickets chirping, birds singing, the wind gently rustling leaves.

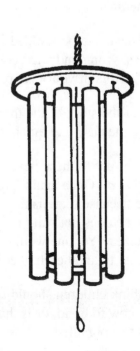

Some things can be mellifluous to you and not to others. Would everyone find the sound of bees buzzing mellifluous? How about children playing?

Mellow means that something is well aged and pleasantly mild, made gentle with experience. Do you think that mellow people find more things mellifluous, or do you think that hearing mellifluous things makes people mellow? Can you answer that conundrum?

petty

If something is *petty*, it is not important. Petty things are small and minor.

When people complain about little things like their piece of cake just being a tiny bit smaller than everyone else's or having to wash one more dish than their sister, they are complaining about petty things. They are behaving in a petty way. When one behaves in a petty way, he or she is acting with narrowness and meanness.

Can you think of a time when someone was acting petty? How about when someone refused to lend you a pencil although he or she had five of his or her own? How about when someone teased you because you added a number wrong?

Has anyone ever said to you, "Don't be so petty!"? Would it be easier to like a petty person or one who "doesn't sweat the small stuff"?

Have you ever thought that worrying about correct punctuation is petty? Yet look at how punctuation changes the meaning of these sentences: Come here and look at this. Come here and look at this! Come here and look at this?

If one is not petty, one is not pretty! Isn't it funny how just putting in one extra letter, like an "r" in *petty* to make it *pretty*, can change the meaning of a word so much? In this case, is the letter "r" petty, or important?

upbraid

The *up* in *upbraid* would make one think that upbraid is probably a positive word. The prefix *up* makes one think that one would want to be upbraided. Don't be tricked! English is a tricky language, and though there are many words that give hints as to what they mean by how they sound, *upbraid* is not one of them.

Upbraid means to be scolded severely, to be criticized. If one has been upbraided, one has been told he or she was wrong and was scolded and criticized. If one cheats on a test, one is upbraided. What are some behaviors in your classroom that earn an upbraiding?

Remember the story of the three little pigs? Do you think the first two pigs should have been upbraided for taking the easy and quick way out when it came to building their houses?

Listen carefully to these next two words: *upbraided* and *upgraded*. Once again, proof that one must be articulate because there is no such thing as a petty sound! One does not want to be upbraided, scolded and criticized. Yet one would love to be upgraded, to be put up to another, higher level.

Do you think children should be upbraided for not knowing how to braid, or is that a petty thing for which to be upbraided?

scintillating

Scintillating. From the sound alone, would you like to be scintillating? Do you think it is a positive thing to be scintillating? *Scintillating* sounds a lot better than *trudge* and *irked* and *serpentine*, but is it a trick word like *upbraid*? Use this rhyme to help you decide:

> *Clever young Sue possessed a scintillating wit.*
> *With sparkling fun our lives she lit.*
> *She'd tell a tale with brilliant ease*
> *And bring us laughing to our knees.*

If someone is scintillating, one is sparkling and has a brilliant wit. One is lively and vivacious, sending off sparks. If someone has a scintillating personality, it is as if he or she is throwing off sparks from being so lively and clever.

Would you rather sit on a bus next to someone who is scintillating or lethargic? How about at dinner? How about if you were trying to read?

Are there different times of the days where you feel more scintillating than others? Are there times when even a scintillating person would trudge? Is a hummingbird scintillating when compared to a vulture? Do you find this riddle scintillating: How far can a dog go into the woods? Only to the center. Then he starts out again.

voracious

If one has a *voracious* appetite, one eats and eats and eats and eats and eats. A voracious eater is one who can never be satisfied. It is thought that the Tyrannosaurus Rex was a voracious hunter, one that hunted greedily.

Grasshoppers can voraciously descend on farmers' fields where they can eat until there is nothing left. You may feel like eating voraciously after doing a lot of physical activity or after not eating for a long time.

One can be a voracious reader, reading everything that one can. Some people are voracious collectors of certain cards or autographs. Do you think a voracious riddle collector would like these riddles for his collection: Your pocket is empty yet there is something in it. What could it be? A hole; What question may you never answer yes to? Are you asleep?; What can you hold in your left hand that you can't hold in your right hand? Your right elbow; What should you always keep because nobody else wants it? Your temper.

The *voro* in *voracious* is a Latin root that means to devour, to eat greedily, and you will see it again in other words, so watch for it.

incognito

Have you ever traveled *incognito*? Spies travel incognito all the time. When one is incognito, one is not known; one is traveling in disguise. *In,* of course, means not, and *cog* refers to the mind and thinking. If one is cogitating, one is thinking. When one is cognizant, one is knowing and aware. If one is incognito, one is not known. Do you think that a highly cognizant, knowing person would be able to pick out those who were traveling incognito?

Famous movie stars often travel incognito. They put on fake beards or large dark sunglasses. Years ago, when women were not allowed to be doctors, there were some women who went to medical schools incognito, dressed as men. Do you think that you could travel incognito as a member of the opposite sex? How long would you cogitate, or think, about what your disguise should be? What would be your name be while you were living incognito?

acute

Have you ever had an acute pain? An acute pain is in one sharp, specific place; an acute pain is not an allover achy pain like one gets when he or she has the flu. An acute pain might happen if you hit your knee against your desk, scrape your elbow on the pavement, or get knocked in the nose by a baseball. Appendicitis produces acute pain.

Ac means sharp, and the word *acute* means sharp and pointed. This word, then, also applies to angles. Angles that are less than 90° are acute. They are sharp and pointed angles. Can you draw some acute angles in the air?

Acid has the *ac* root, and acid is sharp and burning. An acrid smell is one that is sharp and powerful, like the smell of burning rubber or spilled gasoline. An acrimonious argument is one that is sharp and bitter.

People who cannot hear can often develop an acute feel for movement; they can tell by the vibrations they feel in their feet that people are cheering. There are people who are blind but have developed an acute sense of light; they can sense with their skin whether a light is on or whether they are by a window.

If one has an acute sense of direction, one never gets lost. The arctic tern, a champion migrating bird, travels 36,000 kilometers each year in its journey from north to south and back again, but it never gets lost. Think of the acute sense of direction of the albatross, a bird that can go for days over the open ocean, with no sign of land anywhere.

What are things we use to help our visual acuity? (Glasses, binoculars, telescopes, magnifying glasses, microscopes)

wax

How many of you thought of floors or candles when you heard the word *wax*? The definition of wax we're going to learn today has nothing at all to do with floor wax. One could get in some pretty funny situations if they thought the word *wax* had only one meaning!

When something waxes, it gets bigger. When the moon is waxing, it is getting larger; every night there is more for us to see. At slumber parties, as scarier and scarier ghosts stories are told, our fears can wax to the point where we have trouble falling asleep. A runner's strength waxes as he builds up his endurance, running further every day. Have you ever heard someone talking, and his or her words just seem to wax on and on?

When something is on the wax, it is increasing and growing. The woman who led the first women's expedition to climb the mountain Annapurna (the world's 11th highest peak) waxed her strength by running up and down big hills with a pack on her back filled with heavy bricks that constantly shifted and knocked against her. Was this a better way to prepare for her climb than working out in a gym?

Whom do your friends wax on and on about—a movie star, the prince of England, an athlete, a teacher? Wax on with your answers!

wane

Wane and *wax* are opposites. When something is waning, it is growing smaller. The moon, when it is not waxing or full, wanes. The moon is growing smaller as it wanes. One's appetite may be voracious, but it may begin to wane after eating several pieces of pizza. One may feel his or her energy wane after having stayed up too long listening to friends wax on about ghosts.

There are commercials on television that advertise that their product has energy that lasts longer and doesn't wane as fast as other products. There are other commercials selling things to help you gain back or keep your strength after it has waned. Politicians worry about their popularity waning in the polls because they might not win the next election.

It is said that in one's youth, an adult, usually one's mother, has the most influence; as one grows, mother's influence wanes while the influence of one's peers or friends waxes. Do you think this is true?

Can one's dislike of unsalted peanut butter and anchovy pizza ever wane?

cosmopolitan

Listen to this poem to help you figure out what *cosmopolitan* means:

> *Felipe Jackson met his match*
> *With cosmopolitan, worldly Max.*
> *No matter where Felipe had been,*
> *Max had already traveled and seen.*
> *But both men read books galore,*
> *And Felipe and Max learned even more.*

The cosmos is the universe, and a cosmologist studies cosmology, the study that deals with the beginning and structure of the universe. A cosmopolitan person, then, is one who is worldly. A cosmopolitan traveler is one who has traveled to many countries, perhaps even to China's Great Wall, the only manmade object that can be seen from outer space.

A cosmopolitan person is one who is at home everywhere and is free from prejudice. Some cities are considered more cosmopolitan than others. San Francisco, Chicago, Los Angeles, and New York City are all considered great cosmopolises. Would you consider your school a cosmopolitan school? Which would you prefer: becoming a cosmopolitan traveler or a cosmopolitan eater?

ferret

Does anyone know someone who has a ferret for a pet? Some people think that ferrets, also called European polecats, look a little like weasels. Ferrets are used for hunting. Ferrets are active and persistent searchers. Ferrets do not like to give up their hunting until they have found what they were seeking.

The word *ferret* is not used just for the animal. We now use *ferret* to describe someone who has the personality of the animal. When someone ferrets out an answer, he or she is searching for the answer. Detectives ferret the truth. Journalists ferret what is happening in the world and then report it to us.

Can you ferret the answer to this question: Why do you always find a lost object in the very last place you look for it? Did you ferret this answer: Because when you find it, you stop looking for it.

Here is another difficult puzzle for which the answer will have to be ferreted: It can't go up the chimney up, but comes up the chimney down. It can't come down the chimney up, but comes down the chimney down. What is it? An umbrella!

44

amble

Amble has to do with walking, like the word *trudge*, but when one ambles, one is not necessarily tired. Ambling is walking along aimlessly, strolling in a relaxed way. When one is ambling, one is just walking in a leisurely way, perhaps looking in store windows, listening to the birds, or considering the flowers. If you are in a hurry, the last thing you want to do is to be walking at an amble.

Most of you know what an ambulance is, and you might have been thinking, ambulances certainly don't amble! Ambulances speed through red lights, and they go as fast as they can. How, then, are *amble* and *ambulance* related?

We need to go back to Latin once again. The root *ambulo* means "to walk," and an ambulance got its name because originally an ambulance was made up of two stretcher-bearers who would walk off the battlefield with the wounded soldiers. Ambulances certainly have changed!

In England a baby stroller is called a perambulator. Do you hear the root *ambulo* in this word?

If I told you that *somnus* means sleep, what do you think *somnambulism* means? *Somnambulism* means walking in one's sleep. Have you ever somnambulated? Do you know anyone who has? Can somnambulating be dangerous?

parsimonious

Can you get a feel for *parsimonious*—whether it is a positive or negative word—from the way it sounds? Parsimonious. How many of you would like to be parsimonious? Keeping that tally in mind, vote again after listening to this poem:

> *Priscilla was parsimonious with her money,*
> *Stingy to the point of being funny.*
> *No one asked her for donations,*
> *as she was much too concerned with keeping her station.*

What is your vote now? How many people would like to be parsimonious? Would a parsimonious person be generous or not? A parsimonious person would not be generous; he or she would not give things away freely. Parsimonious people would keep things to themselves. Parsimonious people are stingy; they do not give money away. They keep their money and avoid spending it.

A parsimonious person is one who uses crumpled newspaper to clean windows, rather than spray cleaner and paper towels. A parsimonious person cuts buttons from clothing and saves them for emergency replacements or brings home lemon wedges from a restaurant in order not to have to buy lemons. Can you think of anyone who is parsimonious? How do you know?

pod

How many of you are thinking, "This is ludicrous, we all know what a pod is. We know all about pea pods, bean pods, and all those other dry fruits that split open when they are ripe. Pod. Such an easy word." But *pod* is a word that has more meanings than it has letters. Does this seem sensible?

Think of a pea pod. A pea pod is like a container, and two of the other meanings relate to this idea. On spacecraft, the container or compartment that is detachable—the part that can come loose—is a pod. Men or equipment can travel in the pod and then return to the main ship. Pods have also been built for undersea exploration. Pods are on airplanes, too. The pod is a compartment underneath a jet for an engine or for gas. Why do you think they would make a pod for an engine or fuel?

Now for another meaning for *pod*. This meaning has nothing to do with peas or spacecraft. A pod is a group of whales. A pod is a group of dolphins, seals, or sea lions, as well. Where do you think this definition comes from? Do you think that because whales often stay together in groups that it seems as if they were contained, as if they were in a pod?

When dolphins are attacked by killer whales, all the young dolphins are put in the middle of the group, and the adults swim around them to protect them. The dolphins swim in groups, or pods, for safety. Their young can be protected when they stay in pods. Do you know the names for the groups below:

Animal	Group Name
cows	herd
flying geese	flock
sitting geese	gaggle
wolves	pack
bees	swarm
dogs	pack
elephants	herd
lions	pride
sheep	flock
whales	pod
dolphins	pod

How many of you have ever seen a pod of whales?

levity

Here is a hint for learning the meaning of the word *levity*: elevator has the root *lev,* too, and *lev* comes from *levis,* the root meaning "light." Think about elevators. They treat one as if one were very light, and they lift one up. As for the meaning of levity, if one acts with great levity, one is not being serious. One is taking the situation with lightness, with a sense of fun and humor. He or she is feeling up.

When something levitates, it rises. It is as if the object is so light that it can float. Magicians perform tricks wherein people appear to levitate. They seem to float in the air because they are so light.

Baking soda and baking powder are leavening agents people use for baking. Try to make a cake or bread without leaven, and the batter and dough do not rise. They come out flatter than a pancake!

Levity is all right some of the time, but at other times it is inappropriate. Should one approach one's grades with an attitude of levity? If one goes to a silly movie, should one go in with a serious attitude or one of levity? If school is canceled due to weather conditions, who do you think accepts the situation with the most levity: the students, the teachers, or the parents?

Is it appropriate to display levity in a courtroom? How about at a circus?

If one did not read these riddles with a sense of levity, would one find them stupid instead of silly and funny?

What does a 200 pound mouse say? Answer: Here kitty, kitty, kitty!

Where was George Washington when the lights went out? Answer: In the dark.

How well do you know your history? Where was the Declaration of Independence signed? Answer: At the bottom!

Ready for a problem? A rooster lays an egg on the top of the barn. The roof slopes down at a 15 degree angle, but there is an extremely strong wind blowing at 42 knots in the opposite direction of the slope. Is the force of the wind strong enough to keep the egg from rolling off the roof? If you take this problem seriously, with no sense of levity, and begin to worry about what force a knot has and how steep a 15 degree angle is, you will miss the fact that roosters cannot lay eggs!

alleviate

Word detectives, alert! What do the words *alleviate* and *levity* have in common? If you thought of the Latin root, *lev,* which means light, you are right.

Alleviate means to lighten, to make something easier to do or to be endured. Perhaps your homework hours are alleviated by the teacher postponing a test.

The dangers of contracting small pox have been alleviated because almost everyone has been vaccinated, and there have not been any new cases for years. It is believed that the virus that causes small pox exists now only under locked conditions in two scientific labs. Some people think these samples should be destroyed, others that they should be kept for further study. This poses an interesting conundrum, doesn't it?

Do you think one day we will learn how to alleviate, or make it easier to endure, the symptoms of the common cold? How about alleviating, or lessening, the pain from migraine headaches? If someone had logophobia (the fear of words), how do you think a teacher could help that person to alleviate his or her fears? If someone had climacophobia (the fear of stairs), do you think riding in elevators would alleviate that person's fears? How in the world would you alleviate the fears of someone afflicted with cacophobia (the fear of ugliness)? Many people have triskaidekaphobia (the fear of the number 13). Many hotel owners have alleviated any problems with triskaidekaphobia by anticipating these fears: Step into an elevator in almost any hotel, and there is no thirteenth floor! The numbers go from 12 to 14, as if the number 13 did not exist.

Think about how far apart in the dictionary are the words *alleviate* and *levity*. The word *alleviate* is being presented in a different week than the word *levity* for a reason. It is important to realize that Latin roots or parts of words can show up at the beginning, middle, or end of a word and still help determine what the word means.

We have an incredibly complex and complicated language, yet underneath many seemingly difficult words there is a beautiful simplicity. Has your fear of not being able to learn new words now been alleviated?

48

urbane

Depending on where you live, you might think that the word *urbane* has an unfair definition. You may think that the word *urbane* helps give negative stereotypes or ideas about certain people. Are you ready to learn its meaning?

If one is urbane, one is courteous, polite, polished, and suave. Urbane people know what silverware to use, that is, they know to use their eating utensils from the outside in, and that forks always go on the left—except for the very small fish fork. Urbane people know not to blow their noses at the table. Urbane people always wear the correct clothes and have the perfect accessories for each and every outfit. No matter what happens, their manners are impeccable. So why do some people think that the word *urbane* is unfair? We have to take the "e" off of urbane to come up with the word *urban*. *Urban* means "of the city." People are classified as living in urban (city) areas or rural (out of the city, on farms or ranches, etc.) areas. An urbanite is one who lives in the city. If a place becomes urbanized, it is becoming like a city and taking on the characteristics of an urban place.

The word *urbane* originated with the notion that city dwellers are more courteous, polite, polished, and suave than noncity dwellers. Rural dwellers, also known in slang as hicks or hayseeds, were thought to be people who wouldn't recognize a handkerchief if they saw one; if there was a cloth napkin on the table, they might consider using it to blow their noses. Country folk were not considered to be polished or urbane.

Are there urbane people today in the city? Yes. Are there urbane people living in rural areas? Yes. Are there people who are not urbane living in both urban and rural areas? Yes, because no matter where one is there will always be people who talk with their mouths are full or make rude noises at the table.

A question to ponder or think about: If one is urbane, is one necessarily kind?

Einstein (famous for $E = mc^2$) is considered to be one of the greatest scientists who ever lived, and he was not urbane. Once, while he was writing down some formulas he ran out of paper, so he just continued writing on the coffee table! Can you think of other famous people who are not very urbane? How about some who are?

altruistic

Jimmy and Rosalyn Carter are good examples of *altruistic* people. When the Carter presidency ended, they worked together for Habitat for Humanity. There are many altruistic people who volunteer for this organization, which builds homes for families who live in poor neighborhoods. Jimmy and Rosalyn Carter and the volunteers are are concerned about other people; they are altruistic. Altruistic people practice altruism, the practice of taking care of others. An altruistic act is one that is done to help someone else. Holding a door open for someone, giving someone your seat, or helping someone pick up something he or she has dropped are all altruistic things one can do throughout the day. Just telling someone that he or she is doing a great job often makes people feel better, and saying those kind words is altruistic.

Like the Carters, Mother Teresa was altruistic, as was Supreme Court Justice Thurgood Marshall. Can you think of some other altruistic people?

Thurgood Marshall

Alter is the root for "other" in Latin, and altruistic people are concerned for others. We have many altruistic programs in our country. One of them brings hot meals to house-bound people, and others provide free vaccinations. One altruistic program works with adults who cannot read. What altruistic things can you do today?

embolden

To *embolden* someone is to inspire him or her with courage. When you are emboldened, you are given courage. You are made bold. When one is bold, one is brave and intrepid, and when one is emboldened, one is inspired to be bold, brave, and intrepid. George Washington emboldened his men during the Revolutionary War by his courage and his attitude. Sometimes just telling people that they can do a difficult task is enough to embolden them. Often times, when it comes to trying new things, people need to be encouraged and emboldened.

George Washington

New math concepts are often difficult, and many students can't apply what they've learned because they are afraid to fail. Students should embolden themselves with the thought that if they practice and are patient, they will learn the new concept and be able to try new problems.

How can one embolden someone who is suffering from plutophobia, the fear of wealth? How do parents embolden their children when they suffer from brontophobia, the fear of thunder? How could one embolden someone who has phonophobia, the fear of voices? What positive messages would make someone with fears become intrepid?

omnivorous

Omnivorous eaters eat everything: meat, plants, herbs, fish, insects, anything that can be digested. Carnivorous eaters, on the other hand, eat only meat. Herbivorous eaters eat only plants. We are omnivorous; we are not specialized herbivores like the koala bear that can only eat certain types of eucalyptus trees. Thinking of koala bears, do you think it is easier for a zoo to keep an omnivorous animal or one like a koala bear?

Omnivorous, carnivorous, and herbivorous all have the root *voro* in common. *Voro* is Latin and means "to devour," or eat greedily. We saw the root *voro* in the word *voracious*, which means devouring one's food.

Omnivorous, carnivorous, and herbivorous have the root *voro* in common, but what is different about them is how they begin, with the roots *omni, carn,* and *herb.* Once again Latin comes into play. *Omni* means "all," and omnivorous creatures eat all. *Carn* means "flesh," and carnivores eat flesh. *Herb* refers to plants, and herbivores eat plants.

Omnivorous eaters devour or greedily eat everything. One of the most famous omnivorous animals is the great white shark. Over the years, entire kegs of nails, treasure chests, and even a suit of armor have been found in the stomachs of great whites.

Omnivorous does not refer only to food. One can be omnivorous about other things, too. If one is an omnivorous reader, one reads everything, devouring every book one can get their hands on. Fiction, science fiction, biography, historical—it does not matter. An omnivorous music listener may listen to all types of music: rock and roll, country, classical, hip hop, folk, jazz, and blues.

What about you? Are you omnivorous when it comes to dessert?

audacious

A teacher asks students to write an essay on courage. All the papers turned in are about two pages long, except for one student's assignment, whose essay has only one line. It reads, "This is courage." Now this is one audacious student!

Audacious means daring and bold. An audacious haircut may be buzzed on one side, long on the other, and striped green down the middle. Audacious skaters ride their boards down steps and across huge breaks in sidewalks.

It is not just people who can behave audaciously. An audacious theory may be one that is new and goes against previous beliefs. It was once an audacious idea that the earth moved around the sun, not the sun around the earth.

There are some mountain climbers who do not climb with ropes to protect them if they fall. They are audacious climbers, climbing with audacity. Some think that this type of audacious climbing, where a fall means certain death, is foolish. Can you think of something audacious but not foolish?

glutton

Glutton. Glutton. Think about the way *glutton* sounds. In which case do you think the word *glutton* fits better or is more appropriate: a cute puppy that is rolling around on the ground merrily chasing its tail, or a puppy with its mouth full of slimy paper from a fast food hamburger that it found lying on the ground? In which case is the puppy being a glutton?

A glutton is someone who can never get enough. A gluttonous eater will eat 17 cookies, three sandwiches, 16 slices of pizza, 14 candy bars, a gallon of soda pop, and then ask for more. One person may be a glutton only for pizza. Someone else may be a glutton only for ice cream.

You may feel that a particular teacher is a glutton for homework—he or she can never give enough! Some people may be gluttons for pain; they love to give it (like the coach who wants you to do 100 sit-ups in under a minute) or they may inflict it on themselves, running a triathlon which involves swimming, riding a bike, and running. If someone keeps getting into trouble, one might say, "That person is a glutton for punishment."

If there is a glut on the market of a particular item, there is a large amount of it. When the fish market is glutted, there are so many fish that fisherman cannot sell the fish they catch. When an item becomes popular, every store may stock it, and there becomes a glut. Yo-yos come in and out of fashion; one year there may be a glut of them, and then they seem to disappear for a while. There is a glut of commercials on television, and in some cases it often seems that there are more commercials than shows!

Shigeru Iwasaki somersaulted backwards for 50 meters in just 10.8 seconds, and Alan Rumbell did 8,151 one armed push-ups in five hours. Would you consider either of these two men gluttons for punishment?

Are any of you interested in buying dinner for a glutton?

chronic

Once there was a child who would get up every morning and complain about his breakfast. Either the child's mother had made a scrambled egg when the child wanted it fried, or mother his made a fried egg when the child wanted it scrambled. One day, his mother secretly prepared both types of eggs. She handed the child the scrambled egg, and the child began to say, "I wanted fried." Mother said, "I thought you might," and brought out the fried egg. The child looked at both eggs, one fried, the other scrambled, then cried, "But you scrambled the wrong egg!"

The child was a chronic complainer; that is, the child complained all the time. If something happens chronically, it happens constantly. Chronic bad weather is inclement or bad weather that goes on and on. In the Arctic regions, below zero weather conditions are chronic.

Chronos was the Greek god of time, and sure enough, *chronos* means "time" in Greek. Any word with *chronos* in it usually has something to do with time. If one has a chronic illness, one has an illness that goes on and on. Chronic illnesses are not like colds which last only a few days.

Ships use chronometers (*meter* means "measurement") which are incredibly accurate time pieces. If something is in chronological order, it is presented in the order that it happened. We usually study history in chronological order, from things that happened long ago to things that happened recently. Why do you think it is done this way?

If I told you that *syn* means "together," could you figure out what *synchronize* means? When things are synchronized, they happen at the same time. Ballet dancers and synchronized swimmers have to synchronize their actions so that everything looks just right. Cooks have to synchronize their work so that everything for the meal comes out at the right time; if you got your French fries 20 minutes before your hamburger, you would be a little perturbed or irked.

If you were trying to sleep on a train or a bus, how might you deal with a chronic snorer?

insipid

Listen to this poem and decide if you would like to be insipid.

> *Dull and tasteless, lacking flavor,*
> *Was our man, Insipid Taylor.*
> *Never lively, never sparkling—*
> *Couldn't even get the dogs to barking.*
> *Insipid Taylor simply sat—*
> *Twiddling his thumbs was where it was at.*

Insipid means dull and tasteless. An insipid book is one that puts you to sleep. You may find a particular movie insipid, while other people enjoy it immensely.

Think back to the poem. The poem was perhaps as insipid as the man it described. Could the poem have been a little bit less insipid, or dull, if instead of twiddling two thumbs Taylor twiddled sixteen? Sixteen thumbs would have made you think, what type of creature was Taylor? Was he human or was he an alien from a different galaxy? Sixteen thumbs would have made the poem less boring and dull, or insipid.

You may be wearing an insipid outfit, but with the right shoes or the right jacket, the insipidness may disappear, and the outfit might become downright dapper.

Food can be insipid. Ever had plain noodles? Plain yogurt? Pizza that had no zip?

An insipid explanation for lost homework might be, "My dog ate it." Can you think of an excuse for lost homework which is not as insipid?

Many people are bothered by the music they hear on elevators and in grocery stores. They think the music is insipid or too sweet. Would country or classical be better? How about no music at all?

Would you like to sit next to someone with a scintillating personality or one who has an insipid personality? Do some people appear insipid, when in truth they are just shy?

magnanimous

Which do you think is the more magnanimous gesture: a person who passes the sugar or a person who gives a sandwich to a homeless person? A big hint: Take what you know about the word *magnificent* to help understand this one.

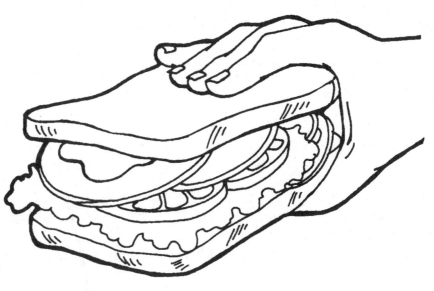

A magnanimous act is one that is big-hearted, generous, and, in some cases, forgiving. Donating blood is a magnanimous act, for it helps people one does not even know. Your sister may break something of yours, and you might say magnanimously, "Don't worry. It could happen to anyone."

Magna means big, large, and great, and so we have the word *magnificent*, meaning something is great. We have *magnify* which means to make larger (for example, a magnifying glass). If something is of great magnitude, it is of a great dimensions. A business magnate is a person with a huge, colossal business.

When people produce something really big or important, like a book or a piece of art, they may feel that it is their *magnus opus*. Their magnus opus is their largest piece of work (*opus* means work).

Behaving magnanimously in this world is often difficult, but it is often the right thing to do. People may magnanimously donate their time or money. On Veterans Day, we honor Americans who magnanimously gave their service to our country. Can you think of a time when someone has been magnanimous to you? Have you ever done anything magnanimous?

literal

If your teacher says, "Settle down! You are acting as if there are ants in your pants!" he or she is not speaking literally. If the teacher were speaking literally, he or she would actually mean exactly what the words said—that there were real ants in your pants.

When something is literal, it is exactly as it was spoken. We have many expressions that we use to create an image, but we do not mean them literally. How about, "I am so excited, I am over the moon," or "I love him so much, my heart is on fire." Is one speaking literally when they say, "I was as cold as ice," or "I kicked him out of my room"?

Many of the cars we make in the United States are sold in other countries. There was one car named Nova, and it did not sell in Mexico at all. When the car manufacturer went to Mexico to figure out why, they realized that *nova* in Spanish, translated literally, means "no go." Would you buy a car with the name "No go"? They changed the name, and then the car sold. Young children often only understand the literal meanings of words. It is only when we are older that we begin to understand the many ways we can say things. If you say, "I am so tired I could sleep forever," that literally means that you would never wake up, but of course what you meant was that you were going to sleep for a longer time than you usually do.

Do you always use the word "cool" literally? Should one always take this expression literally: This needs to be done soon, so can you jump on it right away?

figuratively

The teacher says, "How is the report going?" Your response is, "Oh, we're doing great. It's really flying." If you were speaking literally, you would mean that the report was truly flying, with all those papers levitating above your heads and whizzing across the room. But you were not speaking literally. You were speaking *figuratively*. Figuratively, you meant that the report was going really well and was getting done at a fast rate.

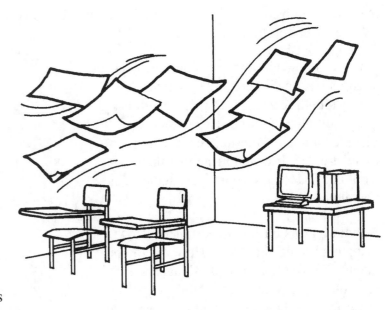

Speaking figuratively is the opposite of speaking literally. Figurative speech creates images to help describe one's feelings. A friend, figuratively speaking, may say to you, "I need to crash." They do not mean they need to get in a car or on a bike and drive into a tree. They do not mean they need to crash literally. They mean to crash figuratively, and that means to stop, to desist, to fall asleep, or to just take a break from everything that is happening.

"He eats like a horse." How does this image differ if one takes it literally versus figuratively? Should these words be taken literally or figuratively?:

> *I'd die for a milkshake.*
>
> *He scared the pants off of me!*
>
> *When she found out that I had not washed the dishes, she bit my head off.*
>
> *You should have seen him! We jumped out from behind the tree, and he came unglued!*
>
> *Boy, she can't sit still today. She must have ants in her pants.*
>
> *She weeps at everything she sees.*
>
> *We couldn't find the keys, and we tore the house apart looking for them.*

Can you figure out what is meant by the following puzzle? (Hint: Do not think figuratively. Think literally!)

> *Land if*
> *Sea if if*

This puzzle uses a literal representation of a famous line from Longfellow's poem, "Paul Revere's Ride": "One if by land, two if by sea." Does anyone know the figurative meaning of this line?

quadruped

We are not quadrupeds! Quadrupeds are four-footed animals like dogs, cats, elephants, or bison. *Quad* means "four," and we have many words where we can find *quad*. A quadrilateral is a four-sided figure. A quadrangle is a four-sided courtyard or enclosure. Does your school have one?

What coin do we use that is a fourth of a dollar? The quarter. A quadrant is how much of a circle? Answer: One fourth, or a 90° arc.

If you can now hit home runs because your strength has quadrupled, by how much has your strength increased? Your strength has been multiplied by four. How would you like the number of mosquitoes in your room to quadruple? It would mean that there would be four times as many mosquitoes as you already have.

A mother gives birth to quadruplets. How many babies did she have? How would you like to change the quadruplets' diapers? If someone says, write your spelling words in quadruplicate, how many times do you need to write each word?

When something happens quadrennially, it happens every four years. What day of the year shows up quadrennially? Answer: February 29.

Quadriplegics are paralyzed in four limbs, both legs and both arms. Some quadriplegics have specialized wheelchairs which they can control with their fingers, neck, or even eye movements.

We are not quadrupeds. We are bipeds. We are bipedal, meaning that we walk on two feet. From this, one can deduce that *bi* means . . . ? Two! How many wheels does a bicycle have? How many languages does a bilingual person speak? Can you create some more words, knowing that:

uni	means one	*unicycle, universe, uniform*
tri	means three	*tricycle, triangle, trio*
quin	means five	*quintuplets, quintuplicate*
hex	means six	*hexagon*
sept	means seven	*septuplets, septennial* (Long ago in a previous calendar system, September used to be the seventh month.)
oct	means eight	*octopus, octave, octagon* (Long ago in a previous calendar system, October used to be the eighth month.)

Sisyphean

Think back to the worst punishment you have ever had. Now compare it to the punishment Sisyphus had to undergo. Sisyphus, a mythological character in the time of ancient Greece, was a man who was condemned to push a colossal boulder up a steep hill. He could not let go of the boulder, for if he did, it would roll back, crushing and killing him. Yet there was no relief for Sisyphus when he reached the top because, at that moment, the boulder would roll back down to the bottom of the hill, and he had to roll it up the hill all over again—forever!

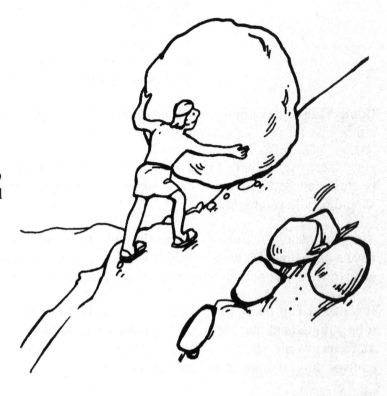

Today, if we have an arduous or difficult job to do that seems to go on forever and forever, we may describe it as a *Sisyphean* task. One will not hear this word that often, but for you logophiles (word lovers), isn't it a magnificent word? What images it creates in our minds!

Learning how to ride a bike may have appeared to be a Sisyphean thing to do when you first started, but hopefully it is easier now. Whistling, snapping, and blowing bubbles may be Sisyphean tasks for some, but quite easy for others.

After a hurricane or a tornado strikes, the chore of cleaning up and restoring electricity often appears Sisyphean, but when people work together and help each other, it is amazing how order can be restored.

If your teacher said, "We have some Sisyphean problems today," would it give you a good feeling about school?

Are these problems Sisyphean?

26 = L. of the A.	*letters of the alphabet*
24 = H. in a D.	*hours in a day*
9 = P. in the S.S.	*planets in the solar system*
8 = S. on a S.S.	*sides on a stop sign*
4 = Q. in a G.	*quarts in a gallon*
90 = D. in a R.A.	*degrees in a right angle*
29 = D. in F. in a L.Y.	*days in February in a leap year*
8 = A. on an O.	*arms on an octopus*
50 = S. on the A.F.	*stars on the American Flag*

equivocate

Equivocating Ellie would say no,
then change to yes,
then back to no.
Because of her way of saying nay, then yes,
Equivocating Ellie was quite a mess.

Could Ellie say a definite yes or a definite no? No, Ellie was *equivocating* and could not be firm in either answer. She kept on going back and forth.

Have there ever been things in your life on which you equivocated? When you ask your parents for permission to go somewhere or do something, do they sometimes equivocate, not sure of whether you should be allowed to go?

The Latin word for equal is *aequus* (in English, we always spell it *equ*) and when you equivocate, you have a hard time deciding because each way you decide seems equal. *Vox* or *vocis* is Latin for "voice," and so when you put them together as in equivocating, you are giving an equal voice to both sides.

If someone is running for office, and you ask him or her what they think about a certain issue, whether it be putting land into parks, putting money into schools, giving children longer school days, or wearing uniforms, would you like it if they equivocated on all their answers? If they did, you could say, "Stop equivocating! I want an unequivocal answer!"

There is a special type of club called a polar bear club. Each winter, when snow is covering the ground and the ocean or lake or stream is icy cold, polar bear club members jump into water and go for a swim. If a polar bear club membership were offered to you, would you equivocate, or would your answer be an unequivocal, "No!"

Here's a story with a conundrum: There was a terrible plane crash on the border of Canada and the United States. On which side should the survivors be buried—the Canadian side or the American side?

You should not have to equivocate, or go back and forth, on your answer. You should have said, "There is nothing to equivocate about. Survivors do not need to be buried."

verbatim

Did you know that there are some people who can simply look at a page in a book and then later recall what was on that page verbatim, without taking a look? Such people have a photographic memory; they can tell you word for word—verbatim—what was on the page.

Are there any poems or songs you know verbatim? Most of you can tell the story of "The Three Little Pigs," but how many of you can tell verbatim the version of the story that was read to you?

Verbs are action words, and a verbal answer is one that is spoken. *Verbum* means "verb" in Latin, and if something has too much verbiage, it has too many words. One can also have a special type of verbiage. Have you noticed that there are particular words associated with computers or certain games that you play? There is computer verbiage (software, hard drive), baseball verbiage (foul, fly ball), or medical verbiage (ICU, post-op).

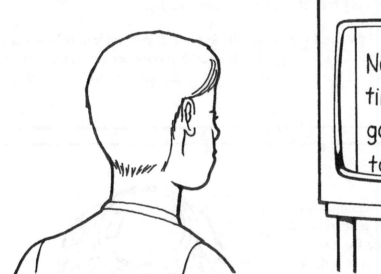

Some people are more verbal than others. Verbal people love their words, whether they are reading, writing, or talking. Not all verbal people can recite things verbatim, though. Also, sometimes people are able to memorize things verbatim, even though they do not understand what they are reciting.

Actors in front of live audiences have to memorize their parts verbatim, but often when shows are being filmed for television, the actors have little TV screens where words flash across them, and the actors only have to read the script. Do you think it would be harder to act for television where one could have the words prompted, or on a stage in front of people, where the actor has to know every word verbatim?

Would it help you if you could recite the dictionary verbatim? The phonebook? A textbook? Can you repeat this tongue twister verbatim?

> *A tutor who tooted the flute*
> *Tried to tutor two tooters to toot.*
> *Said the two to the tutor,*
> *"Is it easier to toot,*
> *Or to tutor two tooters to toot?"*

paternalistic

What are some words people call their fathers that begin with with the letter **p**? Yes, *pa* or *papa* are such words. Believe it or not, the word *pa* is based on Latin. *Pater* or *patris* is Latin for "father," and many words with *pater* or *patri* in them have to do with fatherhood.

If someone is paternalistic, one is being like a father. Some paternalistic behavior is good—taking care of others, keeping people safe, acting like a father. But sometimes patrimonious or paternalistic behavior or attitudes can be quite perturbing. What if someone said, "Oh, women can't be ambulance drivers. The sight of blood would make them ill." We would say that the person who spoke those words was behaving in an old-fashioned, paternalistic, or patrimonious manner.

A patriot is one who loves his country dearly, as if he were a father to his country. Nathan Hale was considered to be a great patriot. He was a young school teacher who was caught in disguise behind the British lines and hanged as a spy in 1776 during the Revolutionary War. It has been said that his last words were that he regretted that he had only one life to lose for his country.

A patriarch is a respected old man, and a patriarchy is where the system of government is based on male inheritance. In England, because it is a patriarchy, girl children can only become queens if there are no boy children to become kings, even if the girls were born first! England is thinking of changing this law. Do you think they should?

alma mater

Not wanting to be paternalistic, a word dealing with *mother* needs to follow so that all things remain equal. One's alma mater is the school or college from which one graduated. How many of you went to or will be going to the same alma mater of your parents or siblings? *Mater* or *matris* (think of the similarity between *pater* and *patris*) both mean "mother" in Latin, and one's alma mater, strictly translated, means one's soul mother, but it has come to mean one's intellectual mother.

A matriarch (compare to patriarch) is like a mother ruler or head of the household. There are some matriarchal societies where everything is inherited through the mother's side of the family—land goes from daughter to daughter. Matrimony is marriage. Mother, daughter, and marriage are all connected. Maternity clothes are for women who are about to become mothers, and a maternal person is one who is motherly. A matron is a person who is supposed to take care of you as if she were your mother. There may be a matron of honor at a wedding or a matron of a boarding school or camp. Notice the similarity between *maternity* and *paternity, maternal* and *paternal*, and *matron* and *patron*.

People often support the sports teams from their alma maters. Will you?

taciturn

Can you use this rhyme to figure out the characteristics of a taciturn person?

> *Taciturn Tony said never a word*
> *And quietly went out to watch for some birds.*
> *Along came an eagle, a raven, a finch.*
> *When there is silence,*
> *Birdwatching's a cinch!*

If one is taciturn, one does not say much. Taciturn people are silent people. If one is taciturn, one is not garrulous.

If you look around at the other people in your class, you will notice that some of you are more taciturn than others. There is nothing wrong with being either taciturn or talkative. People are all different, and it is our differences which make us special. Sometimes people who talk a lot like to be with taciturn people, and sometimes people who are taciturn like to be with people who are garrulous.

Sometimes people will be tactiturn at school, and then when they get home, look out! Words tumble out of their mouths at a mile a minute. Are there some social situations—perhaps when you are first meeting someone—when you are more taciturn than usual?

Take only the first part of the word *taciturn*, and you have the word *tacit*. A tacit agreement is one that is unspoken. It is tacitly understood that when one goes to a movie theater, one will not talk while the show is on. Perhaps there is a tacit arrangement in your family that if someone is on the phone, no one listens in on the conversation.

Because taciturn people are silent, do you think that being a radio disc jockey or sports announcer would be a good job for them? How about a preschool teacher? What if the taciturn person's job was to work in the woods all day counting animal populations or charting tree growth? What if they worked in a lab studying germs and viruses? Would a taciturn person be good for these careers? Why?

sage

Who is the wisest person you know? That wise person is a sage, for a sage is a wise one. A sagacious person, a sage, is one who thinks about things.

A basketball sage would be someone who knows everything about basketball. He or she knows the strengths and weaknesses of every team, player, and coach. Such a person knows a lot about game strategy as well; a basketball sage can predict things about a game that he or she is watching.

A sagacious doctor would be one that knows everything there is to know about medicine. A business man or woman, acting sagaciously, would take wise and careful care of her money. In many cultures, the elderly are considered to be sages, for they have experienced more of life than other people in their community.

In the United States, we expect our Supreme Court justices to be sages. We want them to be sagacious about the law, for they represent the highest court in the land and are appointed for life.

A person who is a sage would know that there is an herb called sage which is used to season food. There is also a plant called sagebrush that inhabits the western United States.

Is there a puzzle sage among you? Can you be sagacious about these puzzles?

36 = I. in a Y.	*inches in a yard*
30 = D.H.S.A.J. and N.	*days hath September, April, June, and November*
1 = D. at a T.	*day at a time*
5 = F. on the H.	*fingers on the hand*
60 = S. in a M.	*seconds in a minute*
16 = O. in a P.	*ounces in a pound*

Now that you know all definitions of the word *sage*, you are quite sagacious about this word.

agile

Though you may not be sure what *agile* means, listen to this poem and then see if you can answer the question which follows.

> *Jonathan Dallas was very agile,*
> *Could bend and twist in fantastic style.*
> *He would kneel on the floor and bend himself back,*
> *Grabbing his heels—with grace that we lack.*

Is an agile person more like stretchy elastic or is an agile person stiff and unbendable like a board? If one is agile, one is able to move quickly and easily. Agile people move with great agility. Agile people can bend and twist.

Monkeys are agile creatures. They can swing and bend and jump from tree to tree. Is a hippopotamus agile? Are some things more agile in the water than they are on land?

Who would you consider the most physically agile: a gymnast, an ice skater, a football player, or a basketball player?

Agility doesn't have to refer to just physical movement. For example, we can say that one has great agility with languages. That means that one can quickly learn new languages and go from one language to another with ease.

If one has great agility when it comes to math, he or she may be able to do all sorts of problems, going from different sorts of problems without any difficulty.

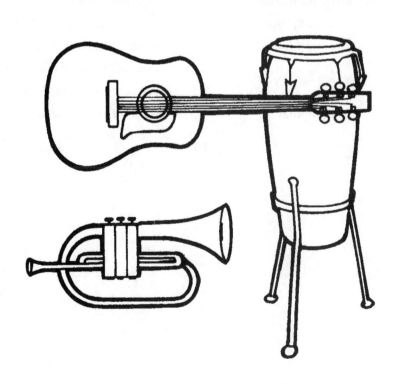

If someone had great musical agility, one could do many different things with music. Perhaps one could play several instruments or write or compose music and sing different types of songs.

How many of you are agile enough to touch your toes without bending your knees? How about putting your palms on the floor in the same way?

circumvent

Years ago, dentists did not have a lot of choice except to pull decayed teeth. If dentists had to pull many teeth, they would fit people with dentures. Then dentists began to stop pulling as many teeth because they learned how to take care of decay by drilling it out and filling the cavities. Yet dentistry has changed today because with proper care, a lot of dental problems have been circumvented. When we brush our teeth, we are circumventing cavities. Dentists help us circumvent dental problems. When you circumvent something, you are making a circle around it, or you are stopping an event from happening by doing something ahead of time or by being clever.

It has been found that when kids have safe, fun places to go, they commit less crimes. Juvenile crime can be circumvented by providing safe places for youth to be with their friends.

Circumvent is actually a great word to know because of its Latin root *circum* which means "circle." When something is circumvented, it is kept going in a circle so that it cannot come to you.

Many infections are circumvented by wearing bandages and washing one's hands. Teachers may try to circumvent any problems students have with substitutes by warning students ahead of time what will happen to them if they misbehave. Parents may circumvent their children from eating too many candy bars by not buying them or keeping them in the house.

Knowing that *circum* means circle, have fun with these words and try to figure out what they mean or how they are connected to circles.

circus	*fun acts in rings*
circumnavigation	*navigating or traveling around something—the world, for instance*
circumambulate	*to circle on foot*
circumference	*distance around a circle*
circulation	*to move around or in a circle; think of your blood circulating through out your body, or think of newspapers circulating around your community*
circumpolar	*found around one of the poles*

steadfast

The wind is blowing at a hundred miles an hour, and everywhere around you objects are being picked up by the wind—chairs, toys, dirt, and even part of a roof. You are holding on as tightly as you can, your knuckles are white and strained, and your fingers feel as if they are being pulled off. Yet there you stay, unmoving, firmly remaining in one place. You are steadfast.

Your friend is accused of cheating. You know that he or she did not cheat, that your friend did well by studying hard. Despite what people say, you do not change your opinion or think that your friend cheated. You remain steadfastly loyal.

When a thing is steadfast, it is firmly attached to one place (like the way a boat should be anchored, or a flagpole should be cemented into the ground). When one is steadfast, one does not change what one believes or what one does. One is loyal.

Do you recognize the Old English root *stede* in steady? When something is steady it is stable, firm, and regular. If you have a steady friend, he or she is a reliable friend. Your friend does not leave you on a whim. If someone keeps you in good stead, they keep you well taken care of. They remain firm and reliable.

The *fast* in steadfast is not the "run as fast as you can" type of fast. It comes from a Middle English root, *fasten,* which means "to fix or focus." When something is held fast, it is held firm and tight. Have you ever heard someone cry out, "Hold fast!" They mean for your to hold on as tightly as you can.

Put the *stead* and *fast* together and you have steadfast. Together they mean holding on firmly without giving up, remaining loyal. Is there a basketball player that you steadfastly believe is the best? How about an actor?

There are still some people today who steadfastly believe that Elvis Presley and Amelia Earhart are still alive. Do you?

Dogs are often called man's best friend. Is this because they are more steadfast than cats?

Amelia Earhart

whimsical

Whimsical. Say *whimsical* three times. Does *whimsical* sound a little musical to you or does *whimsical* sound harsh and hard?

Whimsical is one of those words that sounds a little bit like its meaning. Whimsical sounds playful, almost like the music made by wind chimes when the breeze is lightly blowing. *Whimsical* seems to sort of float off one's tongue in a light way. *Whimsical* actually sounds . . . whimsical!

We use the word *whimsical* to describe behavior that can change at a moment's notice, when we do something without planning, something fun and not serious. When we are behaving whimsically, we are acting on our whims. We are acting on a sudden desire.

A whim is a sudden wish, desire, or change of mind, and so something that is whimsical has this same quality. Something whimsical is unexpected fun. Whimsical things are not planned ahead.

Suppose you were driving down the road, and you are in a hurry to get somewhere. Then you see a sign that advertises free puppies. You pull over and you get a puppy, right there and then. You acted on a whim. You were whimsical. You did not plan to get the puppy. You did it on the spur of the moment.

Or perhaps you are walking down the street, and in a store window you happen to see something that you think your friend will like. You did not plan to buy it ahead of time, but on a whim, you enter the store and get it for your friend. Your whimsical behavior was due to your sudden wish to buy this item for your friend.

When you blow bubbles on a soft breezy day, the bubbles seem to whimsically float, going up a little, back a little, then gently down.

If you were in the middle of reading a long, boring article about plankton, and your teacher, acting on a whim, suddenly said, "Let's do something whimsical," what would you do? Stand on your toes and twirl around? Sing a song? Dance at recess? Roar like a lion?

If, on a whim, you could go anywhere today on a field trip, where would you want your teacher to take you?

insomnia

Are you awake and alert enough to figure out the meaning of the word *insomnia* from this poem?

> *Insomnia plagued little Doug,*
> *He couldn't get to sleep.*
> *Nothing ever helped,*
> *Even counting woolly sheep.*

Insomnia means that you are unable to get to sleep. You may have to get up early the next morning, and you need to fall asleep, but still you twist, turn, and toss. No matter what, you cannot seem to fall asleep.

In means not, and *somnus* means "sleep" in Latin, so if we have insomnia, we can not sleep. The word *somnambulism* was mentioned when you learned the word *amble*, and this word also has *somnus* as a root. *Somnambulism* means sleepwalking.

For some reason, people suffering from insomnia are told to count sheep. Perhaps this is expected to help because it is such a boring thing to do. Why do you think it is sheep we are supposed to count? Were sheep chosen because they all look pretty much alike, whereas cats are all different colors? Perhaps, too, sheep are docile, harmless animals, in contrast to, for example, alligators. Anyone here think it might be helpful to count alligators to make one sleepy?

Cecep, a man from Java, got his picture and name in the *Guinness Book of World Records* because he slept for 15 days in a room shared by 4,000 scorpions. Would being in a room with even a single scorpion make you suffer from insomnia?

avid

Did you ever want anything so much that you would do anything to get it? When you are avid about something, you want it so badly that you are greedy for it. An avid reader cannot stop reading. He or she craves reading. An avid sports fan likes to watch any type of sport any time. An avid traveler may try to go to every country in the world. An avid movie fan goes to see movies over and over. An avid chocolate lover may crave chocolate so avidly that he or she might even eat chocolate-covered ants!

Charles Darwin was an avid collector of beetles. On a collecting trip, Darwin had one beetle in each hand, each a different type that he did not want to let go when he spotted a third beetle. He quickly put one of the beetles in his hand into his mouth so that he could catch the third beetle. Little did he know that the beetle he put into his mouth was a type of bombardier beetle that protects itself by letting lose a horrible burning substance! Needless to say, Darwin ended up losing all three beetles.

Some people are avid collectors of autographs, beanbag animals, or stickers. Is there anything that you avidly collect?

transgress

When you cross a street outside the crosswalk lines, you are *transgressing*, or not following the rules. In some places, this is considered a serious enough transgression that you will be ticketed for jaywalking. In other places this is considered to be such a minor or little transgression that it is ignored. In Berkeley, California, for example, people have been allowed to cross against the light if there is no traffic coming. In this city, citizens who want to keep walking are not transgressing the law.

A transgression happens when you violate or break a command or a law. You also transgress when you go beyond a boundary or a limit. In most classrooms, chewing gum is a transgression. The next time you sit on bubblegum or have it stick to your shoe, you will understand why it is a transgression to chew it in class.

You probably know the *trans* in transgress from the words *transportation* and *transform*. *Trans* means "across," and so when something is transported, it is taken across to somewhere else. When something is transformed, it is taken across to another form. A transgression is when something goes across or over a rule or boundary. Knowing that *trans* means across, try to figure out some of these words:

transcribe: *to make a written copy of something (hint: scribe means write)*

translate: *put into a different language (go across languages)*

transpacific: *going across the Pacific Ocean*

transfusion: *going across from one into another (think of a blood transfusion)*

transient: *passing through or going across a place for only a short period of time*

prodigy

When Mozart was only four years old, he could play the harpsichord, violin, and organ so well that he toured European courts to show off his talent. Mozart was a child *prodigy*. He was a wonder, a highly talented child.

Do you think Michael Jordan was a prodigy? He was always good in sports, but as a young man in high school, his coach, not thinking that Michael could make it as a professional, told him to study math because that was where the money was. Tiger Woods, however, was a child prodigy. From a very young age, he could hit a golf ball with amazing strength and accuracy. There are math prodigies, spelling prodigies, and business prodigies. However, many famous people were not child prodigies. Thomas Edison, one of the most famous inventors of all times (light bulbs and talking movies were just two of the things he invented), was unable to learn as a child in school. His mother withdrew him and took the slow, painstaking job of teaching him at home.

Whether one is a prodigy or not is not important. What is important is that one always keeps trying and never gives up.

innocuous

The black rat snake protects itself by shaking its tail in dry leaves to make the sound of a rattle snake. Yet the black rat snake is a good snake for farmers to have on their farms, as it kills mice and rats and keeps barns clean. Though the black rat snake's sound is imitative of a rattler, it is actually *innocuous*, or harmless. *Innocuous* means harmless.

Some people feel that wearing a green buzz cut is an innocuous way of saying, "I am different." Other people do not find it innocuous. They are offended or upset by it.

Most of you have been inoculated several times. You have been inoculated so that you are protected against measles, chicken pox, diphtheria, and tetanus. Now that you have been inoculated, these diseases are harmless to you.

The Latin root *noceo* means "to injure," and the prefix *in* means not. Notice that innocuous has to do with something that is not harmful. If it is innocuous, it does not cause injury. These roots are also in the word *innocent*, which means that one is not guilty; that is, he or she has not done any harm.

Is staying on a computer all afternoon an innocuous activity?

Can you think of any other animals that appear at first to be harmful but, in reality, are innocuous?

tarry

Listen to this couplet:

Gwendalyn tarried 'til she was tardy,

Took her time and missed the party.

Taking her time made Gwendalyn miss the party. Gwendalyn *tarried*, and when people tarry, they take their time. Then they become tardy because they are slow or they delay in leaving. If you tarry at the mall, you stay there. You remain at the mall.

This definition of *tarry*, of being slow to leave, is easy to remember because it is so close in sound to the word *tardy*. If you tarry, you will be tardy! Note the power of one single letter.

Sometimes at recess you are having such a good time that you don't want to go in when the bell rings and you tarry. Some people tarry when they eat, and they are never done with their food when they are supposed to be.

Have you ever tarried when it came to doing your homework or starting a report? Sometimes when you are at a park with a great water slide, you are having so much fun that you do not want to leave. You tarry, saying, "I will go down just one more time." Then you tarry longer and say, "Oh, just one more time!" You end up tarrying at the water slide all day!

Would you rather tarry at the beach or at an amusement park?

inanimate

The word *inanimate* may sound tough to learn, but it is not. Listen to it again. Inanimate. Inanimate. How many of you can hear the root *anima* in it? Does *anima* remind you of anything? How about animal? An animal is alive, and if something is animate, it is alive.

All cartoons are animated. Cartoons are drawings that seem to come alive. Animated characters can often do things that real humans and things cannot do. Animation is the art of turning drawings into moving pictures.

But *inanimate* has the prefix *in* at the beginning of it. Do you remember that *in* means not? So if something is inanimate, it is not alive. An inanimate object would be something like a rock, your desk, your books, or the building you are in.

Young children often do not yet know the difference between animate and inanimate objects. That is why they need to touch things all the time and why they believe their stuffed animals are real.

Robots and computers are inanimate, but as they become more developed and can be made to look more human, it becomes harder and harder to believe that they are inanimate. It used to be that the sound of the human voice was enough to tell one if something was animate or inanimate. But now we get into some cars and a pleasant voice says, "Please check your seatbelt." Do you think that such a voice makes it more difficult for little children to realize that cars are inanimate, not animate, objects?

Have you ever seen people get frustrated at inanimate objects and blame the inanimate objects for what has gone wrong? They yell, "You stupid car!" or, "This dumb wrench!" Are people really perturbed with the car or the wrench or is it what the people have done with the car or the wrench?

Have you ever been tricked into thinking something was animate when it was actually inanimate, perhaps at night when it was hard to see?

72

toil

To toil is to work long and hard. When the first settlers came west and built their houses by hand from logs, they worked very hard. They toiled over those huge trees they were cutting down. They toiled to raise up the logs into walls without any help.

When the pioneers dug their wells by hand, they toiled. The pioneers did not have the machines and pipes that people use now. They would have to dig out a hole wide enough for them to stand in. When the hole became deeper than they were tall, they would lower themselves into the hole with a rope. They would shovel the dirt into a bucket, and the person who was helping the digger would wheel it up to the top and empty it out. The hole was dug with great effort and toil.

Eventually, the pioneers would carefully lower a bucket with a lighted candle down into the hole before they themselves went down. If the candle did not go out, then it meant that there was enough oxygen for them down in the hole. If the candle went out, they knew that the air was unsafe to breathe. It was only with great toil and effort that they could have a well.

When one is toilworn, one shows the effects of one's toil. For example, if someone dug a hole for a swimming pool by hand on a hot day, when they were done they would look sweaty and tired. They would look toilworn.

When corn is being raised for seed, the tassels of some of the plants have to be pulled out by hand. The workers have to toil under the hot sun with the corn leaves brushing against them. If they do not wear long sleeved shirts, the corn will cut them and they develop a corn rash. They toil long and hard so that we will have good seed for farmers to plant the following year. Every day when they leave the fields, they are toilworn, sweaty and covered in dirt.

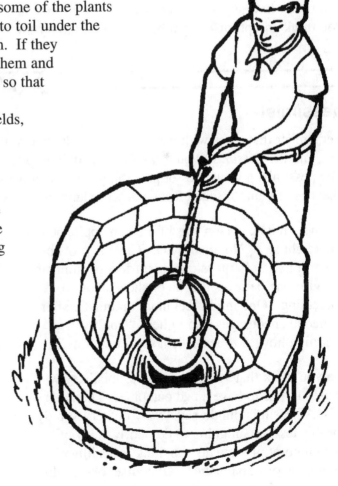

Some people toil at reading because they have a disability that causes letters to appear flipped around, while other people toil at reading because they cannot connect letters with sounds. Yet these same people may find creating art or remembering social studies facts easy. Some people never appear to toil at school work, but they may find social situations much more difficult.

Is there anything at which you toil? What is the hardest thing at which you have ever toiled?

optimist

A glass is filled halfway with water. Is the glass half full or half empty? The answers "half full" or "half empty" refer to the same amount of water, but they are put in a very different light. "Half full" seems to be a positive view, while the other is more negative.

It is said that if you see the glass as being half full, you are an *optimist*. Optimists are people who see things in a good or positive way. When an optimist receives a poor grade on a test, he or she will say, "Now I have lots of room to improve!" If an optimist's cat makes a mess on the rug, he or she will say, "Well, at least I have a cat to look after."

Perhaps your family is going to the beach in a few days. You listen to the weather report, and the announcer says, "A hurricane is coming." An optimist would say, "I am going to be optimistic about this. A lot of hurricanes fizzle out, and there's a good chance everything will be fine."

If you were stuck on a desert island, an island so remote that few, if any, airplanes went overhead, and it was not on a main ship line, would you feel optimistic that you could find a way to be saved? Would you rather have a person there with you who was an optimist or one who was not an optimist? Why do you think an optimist might be more likely to be saved?

pessimist

Remember that glass with water in it up to the half way point? The optimist would say that it is half full, and the *pessimist* would say that it is half empty. The pessimist is the opposite of the optimist. The pessimist always sees or puts things in a negative way. The pessimist would be sure that the chances of being rescued from a desert island, if one were shipwrecked, would be slim to none.

If a pessimistic person was offered an apple, he or she might say, "No, thank you. There is probably a worm in it." Perhaps one might feel pessimistic because one believes that he or she cannot do something. One might feel more optimistic after someone encourages him or her. "Don't worry. Learning how to rollerblade takes a few tries."

Do you think that sometimes a pessimist's view causes things to have a bad outcome? Think of this: A pessimist might say, "Why bother to study for this test? I am going to do poorly anyway." Which point of view do you think is healthier, optimistic or pessimistic? (Of course, one could take the middle road and be a *realist*!)

torpid

Can you figure out from this poem what *torpid* has to do with *torpedo*?

> *Torpid Terry was always lazy,*
> *Used to drive her parents crazy.*
> *Torpid Terry was by a vicious hornet stung—*
> *And like a torpedo did she run!*

If you could not figure out the connection between *torpid* and *torpedo*, do not worry! Most people can't. When one is torpid, one is without energy, and that definition does not seem to connect to a torpedo, a fast moving bomb. But many of our words have interesting histories, and this is one of them.

Torpid means that there is an extreme lack of motion or power or exertion. When a river becomes torpid, it becomes slow moving, almost without current. Torpid movements are sluggish and without energy. When bears hibernate, they are torpid. Their heart beats go down, they breathe slowly, and they do not move.

Now, there is a variety of fish that dart out very quickly and attack their prey by biting. Their bites make their victims torpid—the bitten fish lose all energy and become numb. Because these fish created torpid-like symptoms in their victims, they becames known as "torpedo fish." When the first torpedoes were invented, they were named torpedoes after the torpedo fish.

What makes you feel torpid? Hot weather? Folding laundry?

boisterous

Have you ever been to a game or a parade where all the people in the crowds are yelling, waving their arms, and perhaps even stomping their feet? The crowd is *boisterous*. When one is boisterous, one is boiling over with high spirits and rowdiness. Crowds can become so boisterous at times that they storm the field and tear down goalposts.

Some people are more boisterous than others. They are noisy and excited. The boisterous child may scream and yell and dance a jig if he or she wins a pencil without an eraser, while the non-boisterous child may quietly say, "Oh, by the way, I won a trip to Disneyland."

There are some days when we are more boisterous than other days. For example, often when a class goes on a field trip, the students are more boisterous than usual. People often become boisterous at parties.

Would you like it if you went to see a movie and the crowd in the movie theater was boisterous? Would you expect a crowd to be boisterous if it were the last game of the season, the score was tied, and there were only five minutes left to go?

It has been said that boys are naturally more boisterous than girls. Do you think this is true?

vilify

Vilify is a word that many sound completely new to you when you first hear it, but it is one of those words where you actually know a lot of words that are connected to it.

Vilify is related to the word *evil*; notice the same root, *vil,* in both evil and vilify. Do you think it would be a good thing or a bad thing if you vilified someone? When you vilify someone, you make them evil. You may gossip about them in a mean way. You bring them down by saying bad things about them.

A villain is a person who has done something bad or evil. Superman and Batman always subdue and capture the villains. Villains are evil, and they often try to vilify the good guys.

Many times when people run for a political office like the presidency or the governorship, they vilify their opponents. Do you think this is a proper way to campaign?

Have you ever gotten in a fight with a friend, and before you had everything settled, your friend told everyone nasty things about you? Your friend has vilified you. Do you think good friends should ever vilify each other?

Bats are often seen as vile creatures. They are the villains in horror movies where they attack the heroes. Yet bats are far from being vile or villains. Bats have been vilified unfairly! Bats are the world's most important predators of insects that fly at night. Without bats, we would have a lot more mosquitoes and bugs eating our crops. And did you know that many fruit-eating bats scatter the seeds of some of our favorite fruits? Bats also pollinate trees and shrubs. The next banana you eat may well exist because of a bat.

Vampire bats have been especially vilified. Yet vampire bats are not aggressive or dangerous at all, and they are small enough to fit in the palm of your hand. Vampire bats feed on sleeping animals, usually cows and horses. They land near the animal and walk up to it. After making a small cut in the animal's skin, they lap up some blood. The animal usually never wakes up while the bat is supping upon it.

Wolves are often vilified in story books. Are wolves really the villains they are made out to be? Could one retell the story of "The Three Little Pigs" from the wolf's perspective?

ardent

Try to figure out what the word *ardent* means from this poem:

> *Ardent Andy felt great ardor*
> *For all the things kept in the larder.*
> *His heart longed for sugar and spice,*
> *And everything that tasted nice.*

Ardent Andy felt great ardor for his food. Andy was passionate when it came to eating. He loved food. He was arduous about it.

Ardo means "to burn" in Latin, and so if someone is ardent about someone, he or she feels a burning passion or desire for him or her. Some people are ardent about certain movie stars. They feel great ardor for them and hang their picture up on their wall, join their fan clubs, and read everything that is ever printed about them.

Ardent cooks love to cook. They cook with such passion that their hearts burn hot and fiery about what they are doing. Ardent singers will often join community groups where they can sing all sorts of music. They have a fiery passion for singing.

Have you ever met an ardent collector of baseball cards or beanbag animals? They know everything there is to know about what they are collecting, and they almost burn with desire for the objects they collect. Some stores that sell collectibles for children do not allow people over the age of sixteen to enter when new shipments came in; they found that some adults would jump out of line and shove little children out of their way to get what they wanted. The beanbag animal collectors were certainly ardent about the stuffed animals.

The Chicago Cubs baseball team is known for having ardent supporters. Its supporters feel excited about the Cubs even when the Cubs lose.

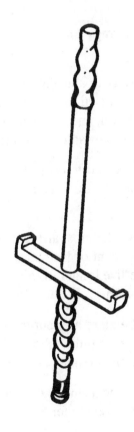

Gary Stewart once jumped 177,737 times non-stop on a pogo stick. Do you think Gary was ardent about pogo stick jumping, or was he just bored and had nothing better to do?

Is there something you feel ardent about—free speech, chocolate cake, school? Is there someone for whom you feel great ardor?

retrospect

When one looks at something in retrospect, one is looking back in time. One looks back and reflects on what has happened. In retrospect, there are many things that you might have done differently. Perhaps you would have started taking musical instrument lessons at an earlier age, or perhaps you would not have been so mean to your sister or brother. *Retro* means backward and *specto* (think of spectacles) means to look. So *retrospect* literally means "looking back."

Sometimes a museum will put on an exhibit that is a retrospective of a particular artist. If this is the case, the museum has put on an exhibit of the artist's work and displayed it in a chronological or historical order. There might be pictures from when the artist was just starting out, from his or her middle years, and from his or her later years. Then people can see how the artist matured or changed over time.

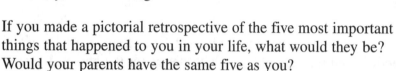

Perhaps someone in your family has made a retrospective photo album that has all of your school pictures starting from kindergarten up to present day. People can see how you have changed. The second grade pictures are usually great to look at—everyone is missing teeth!

If you made a pictorial retrospective of the five most important things that happened to you in your life, what would they be? Would your parents have the same five as you?

affluent

Imagine two people, one in rags and begging for food, the other one in silk clothes and eating caviar. Which one is affluent?

Someone who is affluent has an abundance of things—a great supply, a great wealth, an excess, more than enough. The person dressed in silk and eating caviar is the affluent person. That person is rich. *Fluo* means "to flow" in Latin, and so when someone is affluent, money flows to them. Notice the fluent in *affluent*. *Fluent* means smooth and rapid, as in fluent in languages. Air flows through a flute.

Though individual affluence is often easy to see—swimming pools, expensive cars, and huge houses—there are many individuals who do not show their affluence so openly. Don't judge affluence by appearance!

The United States is one of the most affluent countries in the world. We have a large amount of land and quantities of good natural resources. People live longer in the United States than they do in many other countries. We are an affluent society.

Though one school may be more affluent than another school, when it comes down to winning, the school that has the most spirit and "I can" attitude often comes out ahead.

Having a telephone used to be a sure sign of affluence. Is this so today? How about a car? A computer?

vex

Vex! Just from the sound, is vexed something you would like to be? Would you like to feel vexation? When one is vexed, one is irritated, annoyed, or troubled. One can also be puzzled when vexed. For example, one may find a particular problem vexing.

Do you find this question vexing: Why is it that people always put their right shoe on first? The answer to this riddle can be as vexing as the question because it is so simple: People always put their right shoe on first because it would be foolish to first put on the wrong shoe!

Your mother may be vexed because you did not tell her that you were going to your friend's house. Your teacher may find it vexing that you forgot your homework. You may be vexed at yourself that you forgot your lunch money.

What vexes you? How do you keep yourself from becoming vexed with people you like?

Here are some puzzles that are incredibly vexing. Each one represents a familiar expression we use. Can you figure them out, or are you vexed?

PPOD	*pea in a pod*
iecexcept	*i before e except after c*
WORL	*world without an end*
ankoolger	*look back in anger*
1T345	*tea for two*

tantalize

You can try to get a donkey to move by hanging a carrot on a stick in front of it. The donkey keeps going forward, but it never gets to the carrot. The carrot is tantalizing the donkey. The donkey is tantalized by the carrot.

When something tantalizes you, it is just beyond your reach. You just can't quite reach it, and it keeps teasing you.

Ever opened up a box of chocolates? The creamy candy, in all those pretty shapes, is tantalizing. You want to eat every piece. You find the chocolate tantalizing.

Cats are tantalized by strings dangling in front of them. Older children are known for tantalizing younger children with their favorite toys, just by holding the toys out of reach of the younger children.

The word *tantalize* comes from the mythological Greek god, Tantalus. Tantalus gave some secrets of the gods to humans, and he was punished by having to stand up to his chin in a pool of water. Just above him was a tree with wonderful fruit. Every time he tried to reach the fruit or even take a sip of water, the fruit would move away from him or the water would go down so that he could not drink. Tantalus was tantalized by the water and the fruit.

Good commercials tantalize us so that we run out and buy what we see advertised. What commercials do you find tantalizing?

witty

Listen to this poem to help you decide who is the most witty: a comedian or a doctor, an astronaut or a talk show host?

> *Witty Willy had great wit,*
> *And always was a social hit.*
> *Using words to laugh and play,*
> *He put some fun into our day!*

Though it is true that a doctor or an astronaut may be witty, it is more likely that the comedian or a talk show host will be the one to show the most wit. When one is witty, one uses words in a clever and fun way. Witty people can play with words in an almost silly way, making things funny and amusing. To have wit, to so quickly be able to play humorously on the words that were just spoken, one must be quick thinking. If someone says, "I am cold," a witty person might reply, "Hi, Cold. I'm Brittany." Witty people quickly play with words in a fun manner.

If your teacher said, "Time flies like an arrow," and asked your class what it meant, a witty person might respond seriously, "Ah, yes, and fruit flies like a banana." Can you think of something witty you recently said or heard in class?

assimilate

Look closely at the word *assimilate*. Do you see part of the word *similar* within it? If something is assimilated, it is made similar. When something is assimilated, it is absorbed into or made part of a group.

The United States is made up of people who have many wonderful and different backgrounds. People came to settle in the United States from many other countries around the world. At first, when most people came, they could not speak English, or they did not understand our ways of living. Then, as the years went by and as they had children who went to school with other Americans, these newcomers became more assimilated. They became more like other Americans.

Assimilation works both ways. Not only do individual people become assimilated, but the American way of living can adopt some of the new ways of the new people coming in. For example, tacos, a Mexican food, are considered standard American food now— they can be bought at stands all over the country. Tacos have become assimilated as an American food.

Sometimes people who are new to the United States are afraid that their children will become too assimilated, that their children will forget their parent's language or their history. How can children of newcomers balance their parents' worries with their need to assimilate, or fit in?

valid

A valid argument is a good strong argument. A valid argument makes sense and is justifiable. Valid arguments are convincing and based on good reasoning.

If someone said, "Monkeys like bananas. Because you like bananas you are a monkey," that would not be a valid argument or statement. There would not be validity to that argument.

To make this argument valid, to make it have strength, one would have to prove that indeed only monkeys like bananas. Yet that cannot be proved because lots of other creatures like bananas, including people, elephants, orangutans, and chimpanzees.

Take dinosaurs. Scientists have tried to figure out for years why they became extinct. As more and more evidence is found, some theories lose validity while others become more valid.

When scientists first guessed that our continents were once joined into one mass of land and that, through continental drift, they separated, people laughed. The theory was validated by studying the fossil record and using scientific equipment that could measure small changes. Now the theory of continental drift is considered valid, and students are introduced to it in school. If you think you shouldn't have a test today, could you produce a valid argument to your teacher as to why not? Should children be allowed to watch any movie they desire? Can you produce a valid argument to support this?

frivolous

Have you ever been to a restaurant that places a sprig of parsley on the side of the plate? How about a slice of orange that you didn't order but is on the plate for decoration? Some people consider those side touches frivolous, while other people think they are necessary for the full dining experience.

If something is frivolous, it is not important. It is not serious. If one behaves in a frivolous way, he or she is acting silly and without seriousness.

Young children often consider a milk mustache as frivolous; they could care less if they have one. It is not important to them. Yet when people get older, milk mustaches are not frivolous details. People would be embarrassed if they went to school wearing one.

Likewise, not taking out the garbage or feeding the cat may be a frivolous detail to you, but to your parents and your cat, it most certainly is not!

Making the bed is another thing that divides this world. There are those who think it is a frivolous task while others think it is not frivolous. How many of you consider making a bed frivolous?

potent

Something that is potent is powerful and strong. Smells can be potent. Potent smells can be wonderful, like if we live next to a bakery; they can also be horrible, like the scents that come from certain factories.

Potens (or *potentis*) is Latin for "powerful," and we can find this root in many of the words close in meaning to *potent*. If one has great potential, he or she has a good chance of becoming powerful and strong. Many athletes show good potential, but then they injure themselves or burn out, getting tired of the sport.

Many students have good potential, but because they are troubled or not putting in any effort, their grades do not reflect what is expected of them.

A potion is like a medicine that is supposed to be able to do something. A love potion is supposed to make someone fall in love with you. It is supposed to have a powerful effect. If someone was omnipotent (remember that *omni* means "all"), he or she would be all powerful—the strongest in the world.

Penicillin is a potent medicine. It is very strong and effective and has helped save many lives. Can you think of other potent medicines?

Do some flowers have a more potent scent than others? Which ones?

extricate

You have just sat on gum. How do you extricate yourself?

You did not read the directions, and you have just stuck your fingers together with glue. How do you extricate yourself?

When you are extricated, you are released or freed from whatever it is that is holding you back or tangling you up. *Ex* means "out of" (think of *exit*), and when a splinter is extricated, it is removed or freed from the skin that was holding it in.

Though it happens rarely, children do sometimes fall down old wells or mine shafts. Rescue workers have to be very careful as they extricate the victims, for they do not want them falling even further down the hole.

When bull riders or bucking bronco riders fall off their animals at rodeos, it is a very dangerous time, for the angry animals can stomp on them or gore them. The clown's job is to help these fallen riders extricate themselves from danger. The clowns get the attention of the wild and angry animals by jumping around and acting crazy while the riders extricate themselves by climbing out of the ring.

How would you extricate yourself from this sticky situation: You have told two different friends that you would do something different with each of them—and gave them each the same day and time? What could you do to get out of this fix?

pell-mell

When there is a fire alarm, one is supposed to exit or leave the building in a clear and orderly fashion. One is not supposed to run pell-mell out the doors. When something is pell-mell, it is in a tangled and mixed confusion. It is done in a confused haste.

You are with your friends at a beach, and you are all standing by the water. All of the sudden a colossal wave comes up, and as fast as you can, you try to pick up your towels and lunches and run pell-mell from the shore. You are not fast enough, and the wave tosses and turns your towels and your lunches pell-mell.

There is a great story about the origin of the word *pell-mell*. And no, it is not from Latin. Back in Britain in the 16th century, a game called pall-mall was quite common. In this game, a round ball was struck with a mallet through a curved piece of iron. The winner was the one who had the fewest blows or the number that everyone had agreed upon. During the game of pall-mall, it was quite common for players to run around and thrash wildly, often tripping each other in their efforts to hit the ball. From this, we now use the word *pell-mell* to mean things are in tangled confusion and disorder or in confused haste.

If a mouse appeared right now in the center of the room, would you run pell-mell for the door?

fledgling

Can you get a feel for what the word *fledgling* means from this poem:

> *The fledgling robin began to cry,*
> *"I'm not sure I am ready to fly!*
> *Up into the air I'll go,*
> *And then I'll drop—I know! I know!"*
> *But its newly feathered wings it beat,*
> *And so it rose in the air from its tiny feet.*

Fledglings are young birds with newly developed feathers. Fledglings are just ready for flight or independent activities. (By the way, was this fledgling robin an optimist or a pessimist?)

Though people do not grow feathers like bird fledglings, the term *fledgling* is often applied to people, too. A fledgling is someone who is just beginning or who is inexperienced. A fledgling musician is one who is just beginning to learn how to play. A fledgling high school student may be nervous on his first day. Fledgling travelers often are not sure what to bring and end up packing too many things. Fledgling readers, when asked to read silently, often move their lips as if they were reading out loud.

How many of you skinned your knees when you were fledgling bike riders? Do you think people remain fledgling rollerskaters or fledgling trapeze artists for a longer period of time?

disgruntled

Disgruntled. Just how does the word *disgruntled* sound? Does it sound happy? Would you like to feel disgruntled?

Most people have a negative feeling when they hear the word disgruntled, and it ends up they are right. When one is disgruntled, one is discontent. One is unhappy and ill-humored.

Disgruntled students are students who are not happy. Disgruntled workers may feel that they are not being paid enough. Babies are disgruntled when their diapers are not changed. People may be disgruntled with the weather when it rains nonstop. Many people find barking dogs in the middle of the night disgruntling.

Which one has correct proper usage of English: five plus six is twelve, or five plus six are twelve? No matter which answer you choose, your math teacher will be disgruntled if you do not notice the error in addition. Five plus six is not twelve!

incessant

Bzzzz! Oh, that mosquito that won't leave you alone! Bzzzz! It's enough to drive one crazy! You try covering your ears; you try turning on the light and looking for it, but of course it disappears the minute the light comes on, and though you know you need to get to sleep because you have a big day ahead of you, there it goes again—bzzzz! The whining of that mosquito is incessant. It seems to go on forever and nothing seems to stop it. When something is *incessant*, it does not stop. It is continual. The mosquito's whine is incessant; it is unceasing and continuous.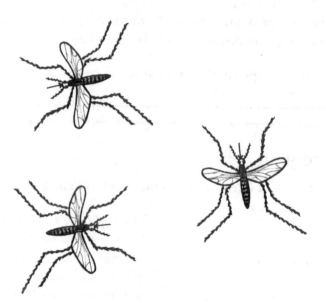

If a baby cries incessantly, it is easy to feel as if you are going to go crazy. The baby never stops crying. Three-year-old children are known for incessantly asking, "Why?" Young children are often plagued with incessant ear infections; they get one ear infection after another.

If you live next to a road, there may be an incessant sound of cars. When a cat has not been fed, it may incessantly scratch at the window screen or meow. Even yelling at it does not stop its continuous and incessant meowing.

A country may have problems with an incessant drought when it does not rain year after year. The drought is continuous, and everything is dry.

Could you learn in a classroom where there is incessant fighting or noise? Could you learn if you had incessant hunger pains?

84

subaqueous

Can you use this rhyme to figure out what *subaqueous* means:

> *The subaqueous squid*
> *Was shy and hid.*
> *If the squid is found*
> *In its watery ground,*
> *It squirts its ink*
> *And is gone in a blink.*

Subaqueous means underwater. Squids are subaqueous creatures because they live in or under the water. Squids shoot a substance that looks like a purplish-black ink for defensive purposes. When squids need to get away from whatever it is that is chasing them, they squirt their ink. By the time the "ink" has cleared, the squid is long gone.

Aqua means "water." Do you hear this root in *aquarium* and *aquatic*, which also have to do with water? The root *sub* means "under," and you can hear that in *submarine*. If something is submersible, it can go under. Something subaqueous goes under water, too.

Some subaqueous creatures are completely blind. They live so far down in the water that light does not penetrate down to them. This is true for some ocean fish and some fish that live in caves in lakes in the middle of the United States! What good would eyes be when there is nothing to see?

Are humans subaqueous? Can they make themselves subaqueous?

emit

You are having a surprise party for a friend. You have been told that, no matter what happens, do not make, or *emit*, a sound. You try not to emit any sounds as you are waiting for your friend to open the door, but the person next to you has just made the funniest face in the world. You cannot help yourself. Stifled giggles are emitted. The giggles are let out.

When something is emitted, it is sent out. The squid emits an ink-like substance for defense. Chimneys emit or discharge smoke. Our bodies emit sweat to keep us cool.

Onions emit such strong odors that our eyes begin to tear. It has been said that putting an onion in the refrigerator before cutting it will reduce the odors emitted and thus the weeping.

Mit means "send," and so when something is emitted, it is sent out, let out, or discharged. To transmit something is to send it across (remember that *trans* means "across" and *mit* means "to send out"). When you submit to something, you are giving yourself to it—you are letting yourself to be placed under something, or even someone. When you omit something, you forget to send it. Should one omit their name on a raffle ticket?

What emits a louder sound: an egg or a water balloon when it breaks on the ground?

tedious

Can you imagine picking strawberries all day long? At first you would eat some strawberries, and you would enjoy being outside, but after a while your back would begin to hurt, and the rows would seem to go on and on in front of you. Picking strawberries all day would become a *tedious* thing to do. It is tedious because you have to do it for so long and because it is boring.

Some people find watching a football game tedious, while other people find watching a game of cricket tedious. Some games of cricket continue for over a week!

Some feel tedium or boredom when they do a tedious job. Washing dishes can be a tedious job, as can be mowing the lawn. Truck drivers listen to the radio or books on tape to keep their jobs from becoming tedious. Brushing your teeth may be tedious, but it is necessary.

What would you find more tedious: counting all the toothpicks in a box or baby-sitting a young child? Washing the car or washing the floor? Writing spelling words 10 times or writing phone numbers 10 times?

cacophony

Do you think a baby just learning to talk could say the word *cacophony*? *Cacophony* is a harsh word to say, and *cacophony* means harsh and discordant sounds. Cacophonous sounds are unpleasant, and they grate on your nerves.

Before a symphony starts playing, all the musicians warm up and tune their instruments—the results are cacophonous. Once the conductor starts the musicians in playing the music, though, the sound is beautiful and melodious. It is no longer cacophonous.

Do you recognize the root *phon* in *cacophony*? *Phon* means "sound," and you can hear it in *telephone* (we know what a telephone is, but if we just looked at word roots, it would mean "sound from afar.") How about saxophone? A saxophone is a musical instrument that makes sounds and was invented by a man named Adolphe Sax. Phonics is the system of putting together sounds and letters or symbols. Many children are taught to read by learning the sounds of letters and syllables, or through phonics.

Have you ever been in the city at night? Sirens blare from ambulances or firetrucks, people yell at each other, horns honk, car tires squeal as brakes are pressed, and everywhere there is sound. It is a cacophony of noise!

The tropical rain forest or jungle is a cacophony of sound, too, but of a different sort: monkeys shrieking, birds calling and twittering, animals growling, rain pounding, water roaring, frogs croaking, and insects buzzing. Do you think you could sleep in a rain forest? How long do you think it would take getting used to such a cacophony?

turbulent

Can you get a feel for the word *turbulent* from this rhyme:

> *Turbulent Toni sped all around,*
> *Pushing and knocking things to the ground.*
> *With mighty winds and lots of force,*
> *Turbulent Toni could knock down a horse!*

Turbulent! Doesn't *turbulent* sound like it has a lot of energy? It does—think of a turbo jet! If something is turbulent, it has a lot of disturbing energy; it is agitated. If something is turbulent, there is a lot of thrashing around, a lot of motion.

How many of you have ever flown? What happens when the plane encounters turbulence? The plane flies through wildly moving air—perhaps because of a storm or the wake of another jet—and the plane begins to shake and roll. The pilot announces that everyone is to remain seated and buckle his or her seatbelts because they are experiencing turbulence.

Sometimes you can see a movie or read a book, and there are turbulent scenes. The scenes are marked with great movement and disturbance. They may be scary or exciting. Which do you prefer?

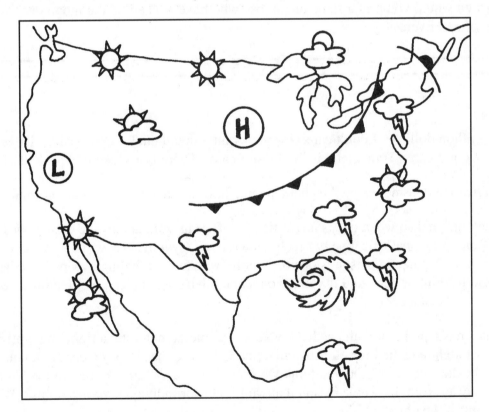

Hurricanes are turbulent storms. Their turbulent winds can knock down walls and tear off roofs. Do you know how turbulent hurricanes are named? Every year the weather service starts at the beginning of the alphabet. The first hurricane of the year starts with the letter "A," the second hurricane of the year starts with "B," the third with "C," and so on. All hurricanes used to be named after females, but then it was decided that was unfair, and so now they alternate male and female names each year.

elite

Winners of Olympic gold medals are an elite group of athletes. They are elite athletes because they are the best of athletes. An *elite* group is a superior group. An elite group is the top or best of a particular group.

Alfred Nobel invented many things, one of them being dynamite. He made a great deal of money from his inventions and decided to create a monetary prize to give to people who invented or contributed in some way to the cause of peace. The men and women who have won the Nobel Peace Prize form an elite group. The winners represent the best in their fields, whether it be literature, medicine, chemistry, or physics.

Sometimes, especially in junior high and high school, certain students will feel that they are part of an elite social group. They feel they are superior to other classmates. They are being *elitist*, feeling that they are better than other groups. Acting as if one is elite solely by belonging to such a group is no guarantee of happiness, however.

We have elite soldiers, elite swimmers, elite teachers, elite musicians, and elite cooks. Those who have been presidents or world leaders make up an elite group.

To what elite group would you prefer to belong, those who have walked on the moon or those who have stood at the top of Mt. Everest?

apathetic

Do you want a million dollars? I don't care. Do you want a doughnut? I don't care. Do you want to go swimming? I don't care. Your friend is ill. I don't care. There is a snake in your bed. I don't care.

If one is *apathetic*, one does not care. Apathetic people have no feelings. They are not interested.

Path means "feeling," and so when one is apathetic, or suffering from apathy, he or she does not have any feelings. If one is sympathetic, one has feelings with you (*sym* means "with"). A sympathetic person feels for you. A pathetic person is one for whom we have sad feelings. A pathetic beggar makes us feel sad for him or her. And if you have mental telepathy, you can feel feelings from a distance (*tele* means "distance").

The United States has a problem with apathetic voters. People do not vote, a right and a privilege that many Americans fought and died for. In Australia, one is fined or has to pay a certain amount of money if he or she does not vote. Do you think we should start a system like that in the United States, or does that take away from the whole reason that we fought for individual voting rights? What should we do to stop political apathy?

feasible

Send a person to the moon? Travel faster than sound? Transplant hearts? Impossible! Not feasible!

At one time, in fact, many people thought these things could not be done, but all of them have been done. These things were, in fact, feasible. When something is *feasible*, it can be done. It is reasonable and likely. A feasible project is one that is capable of being carried out.

Many things that once did not seem feasible are now feasible. Cordless phones once seemed impossible, and now they are feasible. Even car phones are now feasible.

Engineers will do studies to find out where it is most feasible to build a bridge or put in a road. Cities will hire planners to do feasibility studies for new projects and buildings.

Jules Verne wrote about submarines long before any one ever thought they were feasible to construct. Creative and imaginative thinking, as wild as it may seem, is often a necessary step before something becomes feasible.

Do you think it is feasible that there can be perfect attendance in your class for a month? Is it feasible that one day we will be able to speak to a printer and have our words printed out directly, rather than going through a computer? Is there another invention that you think might be feasible?

oscillate

When one *oscillates*, one goes back and forth. One can't decide. Oscillating is like swinging from the pendulum of a clock. To oscillate is to vary, to fluctuate. You increase and decrease, back and forth.

If someone said to you, "Which do you like better, gorillas or lions?" and you, not being able to decide, answered, "Gorillas, no lions, no wait a minute . . . gorillas. Wait, I changed my mind again, I like lions," you would be oscillating.

When some one tries to hypnotize you, you are told to keep your eye on an oscillating object.

The state with the most oscillating weather is Montana. In the same day, they had below zero weather with snow, and then later had sun and 60 degrees!

Here is a question about oscillating: If you were waiting in line to order your food at a restaurant, would you like to be standing behind or in front of people who are oscillating?

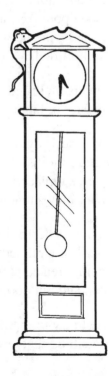

cull

Have you ever bought eggs? Then you know there is a choice between Grade A, Grade AA, Grade AAA, and Jumbo. How do they decide which eggs go in which box? The eggs are sorted and culled. When the eggs are culled, the culler sorts through them and groups them according to size. Sometimes the test for size is to see if the eggs can fit through a particular hole. If they cannot, then they have to be bigger than that size hole; this is part of the job of culling.

Apples are culled, as are tomatoes. The best looking tomatoes are sold as whole tomatoes, and the smaller ones with blemishes are sold for tomato sauce or catsup. What do you think happens to the culled apples? (They are made into applesauce and apple cider.)

When something is culled, it is selected or chosen from a group. Your reading text books are often filled with stories culled from many different writers. Collections of poetry are often culled poems, poems chosen from entire works of authors.

If you were creating a collection of riddles, which one of these would you cull: Why does a cow go over a hill? Because she can't go under it. What did one wall say to the other wall? "Meet you at the corner."

mollify

You put your money into a vending machine, and the machine took your money, but it gave you the wrong soda pop. You are furious. Then your friend puts in her money, and the drink that comes out is not the one he or she wanted, but it so happens that it is the one you wanted! You trade drinks, and you are both mollified.

When one is mollified, one is made to feel better. One's anger has been softened. One feels relief. The intensity of anger or frustration has been reduced.

If a baby's new toy breaks, often just taking his or her attention from it by showing the child a new one is enough to mollify him or her. When people get older though, that is not enough to mollify them. They want a replacement or their money back. If a field trip gets canceled because of stormy weather, the teacher may show movies all day in an attempt to mollify his or her students.

Have you ever heard the expression, "That person is just being mollycoddled?" *Mollify* and *mollycoddle* are related. They both have to do with making things softer. When one is mollycoddled, one is being treated softly; in fact, one is being treated with such softness and giving into that it is ridiculous and not good.

Is it wise to try to mollify an angry dog? How could a zookeeper mollify an angry tiger? If your friend does something that you do not like, can you be mollified?

90

taxidermist

When one goes into a natural history museum, one often sees the work of a taxidermist. A taxidermist practices taxidermy, which is the act of preparing, skinning, and mounting animal skins. Taxidermists are important to our scientific community; the results of their work are studied carefully. Measurements and photographs are taken, and scientists can observe closely different types of beaks, tails, colors, etc.

A woolly mammoth was once found intact in ice. After tests were done on the mammoth's body, a taxidermist was able to stuff the animal so that it could be placed in a museum. The taxidermist helped preserve the skin so that students could learn what animals of long ago looked like when they roamed the earth.

Do you notice the root *derm* in taxidermist? *Derm* means "skin," and you can hear it in *dermatologist* (a doctor of the skin), *hypodermic* (something that goes under the skin, as in a needle), and *pachyderm* (a thick-skinned animal like an elephant or a hippopotamus).

Some biology students have to practice taxidermy on mice. Why do you think mice are good creatures on which to practice taxidermy? (There are plenty of mice, and the tails are difficult. If one can perform taxidermy on a mouse tail, then one is ready for other animals.)

Some people, such as animal rights activists, are offended by the work of the taxidermist. Why might this be so? What do you think?

insatiable

The larva of the Polyphemus moth of North America eats enough food to equal 86,000 times its own birth weight in its first 56 days of life. If we figured this out and compared it in human terms, it would be the same as a seven pound baby eating 300 tons of nourishment! The moth is insatiable. The moth cannot be sated. It eats, and eats, and eats!

The largest banana split ever made was 4.55 miles long, and it was created in Pennsylvania. Do you think even an insatiable eater would become sated, or satisfied, after eating that?

The largest cookie ever made contained more that 3 million chocolate chips. Do you think even an insatiable chocolate lover would get his or her fill?

If someone or something is insatiable, it cannot be satisfied or sated. Do you see the resemblance between *satisfy* and *insatiable*? If something is satiable, it can be sated or satisfied. *In* means not, and so if one is insatiable, one cannot be sated or satisfied. Insatiable readers read everything that they can get their hands on. Insatiable puzzle workers do as many puzzles as they can each day. Insatiable roller coaster riders ride nonstop.

Are people your age more likely to have an insatiable desire for adventure movies or horror movies?

frugal

Listen to this rhyme and then answer this question about Ferris: Would Ferris be likely to buy season basketball tickets?

> *Frugal Ferris was careful what he spent*
> *And particular, too, about money he lent.*
> *Economizing, conserving, and sparing,*
> *Ferris spent frugally and was not daring.*

That was a very difficult question, and both yes and no answers were correct. *Frugal* means sparing, economizing, and being careful of what one spends their money on. Yet being frugal does not mean that one is stingy or mean with one's money. One is just careful with one's money.

If Ferris loved basketball, he might be very frugal with other things he spent his money on—buying an old, used car; buying clothes in a thrift shop or only on sale; never buying brand name foods; and then, because of this frugality, he might just have the money to buy the season basketball tickets his heart desired. If, on the other hand, Ferris felt lukewarm about basketball, he would not spend his money on something he did not really enjoy. That would be extravagant and a waste of money. It would not be frugal.

A frugal gourmet is one who cooks and prepares fancy foods but who makes these foods elegant without a lot of cost. A frugal gourmet substitutes cheaper ingredients for more expensive ones.

How long might you be able to be frugal in order to save enough money for a trip to Disneyland or some other vacation spot?

stoic

Someone gets smashed in the nose with a ball. You know it must hurt terribly, but this person doesn't shed a single tear. Such a person is *stoic*, not showing emotion or feeling. Stoics have restrained responses to pain or distress. Stoics do not show or seem to be affected by passion and feeling.

When the great ship *Titanic* sank, many of the musicians were stoic about their fate. They stoically played their music to the very last. They did not allow their fears or emotions to interfere with their playing.

If someone had a favorite tree or building, it would be hard to be stoic to watch if it had to be destroyed—the tree perhaps because of beetles, and the building because it was a fire hazard. It would be hard not to weep and show emotion as things from your past were destroyed.

There are times when it is good to be stoic and other times when it is all right to show emotions or cry. If you needed a shot, do you think the nurse would prefer you to be stoic about it or hysterical, screaming and yelling? Some people think that boys should be more stoic than girls. Do you think this is fair?

92 © *Teacher Created Materials, Inc.*

marshal

When one hears the word *marshal*, one may think of a fire marshal or a marshal in a western town of years past, his gun slung low on his hip, his hat tipped to women in long skirts, and a silver star on his chest. Yet marshal can also be used in a different way. What does it mean when something is marshaled? What happens when we use *marshal* as a verb, an action word, instead of as a noun, a person, place, or thing?

When one marshals troops, one is arranging them in order. One marshals them and puts them in rank or position. During field trips, for example, the chaperones marshal students in and out of buses and to wherever it is they are going.

At a wedding, the ushers marshal the guests to their seats. They order and arrange where people seat themselves. When there is a disaster, the Red Cross helps marshal rescue efforts, organizing food and aid.

Have you ever seen a sheep dog marshal sheep into a pen? Well-trained sheep dogs seem to know exactly what to do, and even the most stubborn sheep are marshaled back to the fold. Can you think of other things that are marshaled or other jobs in which marshaling occurs?

amass

If there was a contest right now to find out which student has amassed the most paper and junk in his or her desk, who would win? When something is amassed, it is acquired, obtained, bought, collected, earned, or gained. Baked goods are amassed for a sale, creating a huge collection of brownies, cookies, cupcakes, breads, and cakes.

Amass comes from a Latin word meaning "to pile up." When things are amassed, they are collected and accumulated. Something that is massive is really big; it is as if a lot of things have piled up. A massive beast is one that is colossal and enormous, lots of flesh has piled up. A mass of people is a large collection of people. They have not literally piled up on top of each other, but they are close together. When one speaks or thinks of the masses, one is thinking of the ordinary people, those who are in great number.

Some people amass cars, buying all different kinds; others who amass cars prefer to buy a particular type. Hospitals amass, or stockpile, special supplies in case of emergencies. Collectors try to amass whatever it is they are acquiring: stuffed animals, spoons, autographs, cards, or paintings. Think about all the information that a library has amassed. One could read through the many books that the library has amassed and learn bits of trivia, such as the fact that the Egyptians buried their cats with them in their tombs.

Does amassing great wealth guarantee happiness?

prolific

From this rhyme can you figure out what *prolific* means?

> *Prolific Peter painted a lot,*
> *And wrote and played; he would never stop.*
> *New ideas flowed from his mind,*
> *And his products were always the finest kind.*

Prolific means that something it fruitful or fertile. *Prolific* also means that one produces a great amount. Isaac Asimov was a prolific writer; he wrote a great number of books. Leonardo da Vinci, though famous for his paintings *The Last Supper* and the *Mona Lisa*, was not a prolific painter. Today we only have 20 paintings that are credited to him.

Mice are prolific breeders and therefore multiply at a tremendous rate. Rabbits are also known for being prolific.

Pro means "for" or "forward" (think of proceed) and so when one is prolific, one is going forward, making or producing lots of things. A prolific reader is one who reads all the time. A prolific cook is one who cooks many things. Mark McGwire prolifically hit home runs.

Would you rather be a prolific inventor, writer, or artist?

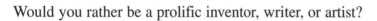

zenith

Can you figure out what *zenith* means from this sentence: "When the sun is at its zenith, I have no shadow." When something is at its zenith, it is at its highest point. When the sun is straight over head, we do not have shadows.

Zenith started off as a word that was used to describe the highest position of stars and other celestial bodies. When the moon is at its zenith, it is at its highest point above us in the sky.

As time went on, zenith went on to be used for other things. For example, when your career is at its zenith, it is at its highest point—you are doing great, and you have reached the top. Sports heroes may have games where they hit or kick or shoot ball after ball. These players are at their zenith. Some players reach their zenith at an early age, and then due to an injury, they may stop playing.

None of you have yet reached your zenith. You all will go far and achieve many things, whether it be by working in or outside of the home. Can you think of some politicians who are no longer at their zenith? (Hint: Think of ex-presidents or world leaders.)

vociferous

Vociferous is a wonderfully pieced-together word. *Vocis* is "voice" in Latin and *fero* is "to bear or carry"; when these roots are combined to make *vociferous*, the word means to carry a great deal of voice. *Vociferous*, then, means noisy, loud and insistent, clamorous and boisterous.

When children play vociferously, they are yelling and screaming, shouting loud and insistent demands or words at each other. If there are cookies missing from the cookie jar, and you are asked if you took them, your answer is a vociferous "No!" You are not shy or quiet about saying that it was not you that swiped the cookies.

One can see or hear the root *vocis* in the word *voice*. The root is also in the word *vocal*, which means "a sound produced by the voice" or "making yourself heard." When monkeys are playing vociferously, they often make great howling vocalizations or sounds.

There have been times at stadiums where the crowds have been so vociferous that players cannot hear each other talk. How do you think the referees feel when they are vociferously booed for making a call that they know is right but that the crowd did not like?

hodgepodge

Isn't *hodgepodge* a great-sounding word? A hodgepodge is a mixture of many things, a jumble. At a garage sale there may be a hodgepodge of items—old bikes, clothes, movies, sunglasses, and even furniture.

Hodgepodge has a wonderful, jumbled-up history of how it came about as a word, too. Back in the 15th century, the French had the word *hocher,* to shake together, and *pot,* meaning pot, which made up the word *hochepot,* which meant a stew made of many different ingredients. A *hochepot* might have potatoes, tomatoes, carrots, turnips, onion, and peas. *Hochepot* became *hotchpotch,* and then finally became the word we use in English, *hodgepodge.*

Sometimes when children serve themselves soft drinks, they like to make a hodgepodge. They put some of every type of drink possible in one cup. A hodgepodge sundae might be fun to make—hot fudge, caramel, and marshmallow toppings on top of five flavors of ice cream.

The United States is made up of a hodgepodge of people. We come from many different countries and cultures to make up a wonderful collection.

Someone might have a hodgepodge of puzzles, and this is one of them: A man was locked in a room that was two stories high. The only way he could get out was the window. Yet the man only had a rope that was one story long. How did he got down safely without any help? (The man unraveled the rope to make two pieces, then tied the two ends together so he could get out.)

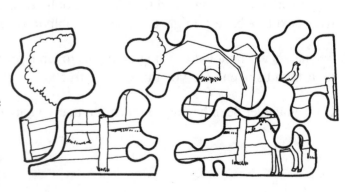

kudos

Do you think *kudos* is a negative or a positive word? It is hard to tell from its strange sound. As peculiar as the word *kudos* seems, it means something good. When an act or person deserves kudos, it is deserving of applause and praises. Kudos are compliments and honors. Kudos, or praises, are given to people who exhibit good sportsmanship, and there is often a special award just for that purpose. Kudos usually go to those people who try their hardest and are honest!

Penmanship and careful speaking is important when it comes to this word, for if one writes or says *kudus* instead of *kudos*, one will be writing or speaking about a large African antelope with long spirally twisted horns. There would be no kudos to the speller who mixes up *kudus* and *kudos*!

The writers of our constitution have received great kudos for their careful thought and wise decisions that went into the document. Kudos to those of you who can figure these out:

56 = S. of the D. of I.	*signers of the Declaration of Independence*
5 = F. on the H.	*fingers on the hand*
9 = I. in a B.G.	*innings in a baseball game*
13 = S. on the A.F.	*stripes on the American flag*

oblivious

"Don't you know it's freezing out there? Put on a jacket before you catch your death of cold!" How many times have you heard that, when the simple reason you did not have a coat on was because you did not feel cold. You were *oblivious* to the cold. When someone is oblivious, that person is unaware or not paying attention. One did not notice the cold. One was oblivious to it and did not feel it.

Young children are known for being oblivious to dirt. Their hands can be covered in dirt, and yet they do not hesitate to use their hands when it comes time to eat. They do not mind or notice the dirt.

Some of you are more oblivious to noise than others. Some of you can do your school work or read, and you are oblivious or do not notice other children walking down the halls, the sounds from other rooms, and what is going on outside the window.

People can be oblivious to certain smells. At first they may notice them, but after a while they stop paying attention to them and they become oblivious. They stop noticing the smells. Someone who lives next to a bakery might even become oblivious to the delicious smell of cinnamon.

Teenagers are famous for being oblivious to table manners, taking enormous bites and chewing with their mouths open. Do you think this is true?

Have you ever been having so much fun that you are oblivious to the time?

versatile

A versatile musician is one who can play many instruments or types of music. A versatile teacher can teach many different subjects or different ages of children. A versatile pilot can fly many different kinds of planes.

If one is versatile, one can change readily. People who have great versatility when it comes to languages may be able to switch from one language to another with ease. *Vers* (or *vert*) means "turn" in Latin, and versatile people can turn to many different things. People who are well-versed are knowledgeable in many different areas; they can speak or write about many topics.

It is not just people who can be versatile. Things and animals can be versatile, too. A hammer is versatile because it can change readily from a tool to knock nails in to one that pulls nails out. It could even be used as a brace, or a small spade in a pinch.

The trunks of elephants are versatile because they can be used for many purposes— smelling objects, picking things up, and carrying water. Birds have versatile toes because they go both backward and forward around a perch. Hummingbirds are versatile fliers because they are the only birds that can fly forward, straight up and down, sideways, and backwards.

Which do you think would be the most versatile tool: the screwdriver or the saw? Would the versatile tool be the better one if you were stuck on a desert island?

antiquated

How many of you have dial phones? Dial phones are pretty much *antiquated*, or out of date. Nowadays most people have push button phones. When something is antiquated, it is as if the thing is an antique, out-of-date and old-fashioned. A dial phone has almost become an antiquity, something of great age from long ago.

Long ago, doctors put leeches on sick people. It was believed that this would help heal them because it would thin their blood. The use of leeches became antiquated, and more modern methods, especially since the development of blood thinning drugs, are now used.

Many people consider Morse code (a system where letters are assigned a combination of dots and dashes or long and short sounds) antiquated. In Morse code, SOS, or the universal "I need help" signal, would be dot-dot-dot, dash-dash-dash, dot-dot-dot. Morse code may seem antiquated in our days of radios and cellular phones, but there are still many times when it becomes the sole form of communication.

Some people feel that because of calculators, adding, subtracting, multiplying, and dividing are antiquated skills, and we do not need to learn them. Do you agree with this?

erudite

If one is *erudite*, one has great knowledge. Erudite people are very learned people. They know many things.

Gauss was an erudite mathematician. He proved many things about number theory and algebra. Gauss once commented that he could add and subtract before he could talk. When he was three years old, he heard his father totaling the worker's payroll incorrectly. Gauss corrected his father!

Newton was also an erudite mathematician. He invented calculus and formulated the three laws of motion which still hold today. "To every action there is an equal and opposite reaction" is one of these laws. Despite his erudition, or great knowledge, when it came to math and science, Newton was known as being absent-minded. Often erudite people appear distracted by reality because they are deep in thought.

One can be erudite about things other than math. One can be erudite when it comes to literature or even a particular author. One could be erudite about cats, a certain country, raising children, teaching, dinosaurs, or the stars. When one writes a report about something, one becomes erudite about that subject through research.

If you could pick any one thing to become erudite in, what would it be?

itinerary

Can you begin to guess what the word *itinerary* means from this sentence: Because he had lost his itinerary, he did not know where he was supposed to be on his next stop.

An itinerary is a route of a journey or a proposed outline of one. For example, your itinerary might be two days in Los Angeles, one day at Disneyland, and three days in San Diego. Your itinerary might have on it whether you are traveling by bus or train or plane. Sometimes due to storm conditions or inclement weather, one's itinerary might have to change.

When someone is holding a meeting, he or she might hand out a sheet of paper with an itinerary or agenda that shows what he or she plans to discuss during the meeting, and in what order. If you are itinerant, you keep moving, going from one place to another. Itinerant farm workers move from crop to crop, going in a particular circuit or order as the crops ripen. Itinerant teachers travel from classroom to classroom, or school to school. Itinerant teachers come to the students, rather than having the students come to them.

If you could go to any country in the world, where would you go and what places to visit would you put on your itinerary? The Gobi Desert? The Sahara Desert? Death Valley? Venice? Paris? Rio de Janeiro? Sydney? Bombay?

What do you think the president's itinerary might look like on a given day?

alacrity

Use this rhyme to help figure out the answer to this question: Do cheetahs move with alacrity?

> *Sarah Foster forgot her book,*
> *So hurried home to take a look.*
> *With alacrity she went,*
> *Taking care her time was well spent.*
> *Sarah returned with book in hand,*
> *Which she returned to the librarian.*

When one moves with alacrity, one is moving quickly and with great speed. One is brisk and cheerful, eager in his or her response. Cheetahs move at great speeds, and they eagerly chase down food. Cheetahs move with great alacrity.

Perhaps one is invited to a party with the letters R.S.V.P. on the invitation. These letters mean that one should call and say whether or not one can make it to the party. They come from the French, *"respondez s'il vous plait,"* which means "respond, if you please." The polite thing to do is to R.S.V.P. with alacrity. You briskly and eagerly say, "Yes, I would love to come."

Your teacher gives you drills on math facts, and with alacrity—quickly and without complaint—you fill in the answer blanks. What other school tasks are usually done with alacrity?

With alacrity, can you name two mammals that do not give live birth? (Answer: the echidna [spiny anteater] and the duck billed platypus)

doff

Do you know the legendary Swiss hero William Tell? In the center of the town in which he lived stood a pole topped with the hat of Gessler, an Austrian. William Tell refused to *doff*, or take off, his hat when he passed this pole because of his pride as a Swiss citizen. For refusing to doff his hat, Tell was ordered to shoot an apple off of the head of his son. In the legend, his son told him that he was not afraid. Tell took one arrow out of his quiver and put it into his belt. He took a second arrow and fit it into his bow. He pulled back with all his strength and shot at the apple on the top of his son's head. He split it exactly in two. When Gessler asked Tell what the first arrow in his belt was for, Tell replied, "That arrow was to put in your heart in case I missed with my second arrow." So much drama for not doffing one's hat!

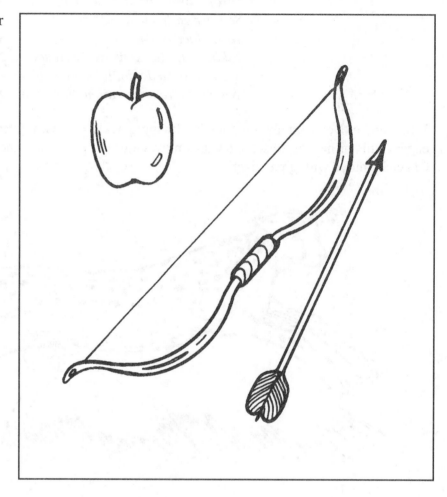

Doff is perhaps an easy word to learn because the word *off* is contained within it, and doff means to take off or to remove. When one doffs a hat, one is lifting it up or off in greeting. If people doff their gloves, they are taking off or removing them.

After hitting a homerun, many baseball players will doff their hats to the crowd. It is a sign of respect, an acknowledgement. One should always doff his hat when entering a building or before sitting down to eat. Even if one is wearing a baseball cap backwards, one should still doff it as a sign of respect when one is greeting someone older than they are. Do you?

egregious

When one first says the word *egregious*, one may think that this is a completely new and very odd-sounding word. Yet *egregious* is a word that one probably knows a lot about already.

One may know the word *congregation* or *congregate*. When people congregate, they gather together in a group, and a congregation is a group of people who congregate. Many groups or churches will refer to themselves as congregations.

When something is segregated, one is kept apart from the group. If there is segregation, groups are kept apart. If someone is gregarious, one likes groups and chooses to be a part of a group. Now, back to *egregious*! *Egregious* has the root *greg* that one also finds in the words *congregation* and *segregation*. *Greg* means "group." But when one is egregious, one is not in the group! Egregious behavior is so conspicuously bad or outlandish that one is outside of the group. Stealing is egregious, as is spitting gum out on the sidewalk. Egregious behavior separates one from the group; it keeps one outside of the group.

What would you consider egregious eating habits or manners? Are some of today's fashions egregious? Will some of these fashions remain egregious, or do you think they will move into the mainstream? Think of how bathing suits have changed. At one time, it was considered egregious for a man to show his chest at the beach.

rupture

Rupt means "to break" in Latin, and a *rupture* is a break. Pipes may rupture, or violently burst, when they freeze. (Remember that ice expands as it freezes!) Later, when it warms up, because the pipes have ruptured or broken apart, they leak, and water floods everywhere.

Sometimes people injure themselves, and they can rupture disks in their backs or tear apart some other body tissues. Ulcers can rupture tissues in the stomach, also.

A friendship can be ruptured, or broken apart, if one friend lies to the other friend. Relationships can be ruptured between countries if one country's leaders lie to another country's leaders or do something that is not liked.

One can hear this same *rupt* root in the word *erupt*. When a volcano erupts, it breaks out. Lava and ash shoot out. When a crowd erupts into cheers or boos, they are breaking out into sound. When something is disrupted, it is broken through or down. Perhaps the peace and quiet in your school was disrupted by a fire alarm. The noise broke, or ruptured, the silence.

Why is it important that we keep boats which are transporting oil from rupturing?

endurance

In 1914 Sir Ernest Shackleton was trying to get to Antarctica so that he could be the first to cross it on foot. He built a ship that could endure or withstand the ice that potentially could crush it, and so he named the ship *Endurance*. If one or something has endurance, one can stand anything. One can last a long time. One endures. One is strong, and one does not break. (What do you think happened to the *Endurance*? You will hear more about it later.)

Athletes will go through endurance training, special training sessions that build up their stamina and strength. Endurance is needed for all sports. Lou Scripa, Jr. once did 70,715 sit ups in 24 hours. Do you have the endurance to do what Lou did?

Some things are hard to endure, to be strong about, and to survive, like earthquakes and floods. With endurance, we can manage to cope with many adversities.

Do you hear the root *dur* in *endurance*? If something is durable, it lasts a long time. Parents like to buy clothes that are durable. They do not want clothes that fall apart soon after they are bought.

Shackleton's ship did not have enough endurance. It was crushed by ten million tons of ice, and his men spent five months floating on ice and surviving by eating any seals and penguins they could find. Eventually the men were able to use their small open boats to reach a tiny island where many of them stayed while Shackleton went for help. One of Shackleton's men was even hunted by a vicious sea leopard, a seal that lives off of other seals. The seal tracked the man by his shadow through the ice and then lunged up out of the water at him! The sea leopard was killed just in time. Shackleton and his men had great endurance. They endured freezing temperatures and dangerous conditions, but they stayed alive and lived to tell one of the greatest survival stories in the world.

Can you think of any other great stories of endurance?

fervent

Have you ever wanted something so badly that it almost hurt? Has your desire been so great that you hardly stand it? If so, your desire was fervent. You felt fervently that you needed something.

If you are fervent about something, you don't just like it—you love it! You love it so much that you have a burning enthusiasm about it. You have great feelings and emotions.

If one has a fervent desire to become a firefighter, one really wants to become a firefighter. One would not want to be anything else. With great fervor, or with intense and burning drive, one would prepare to be a firefighter—doing well in school, keeping one's bodies healthy, and learning all about fires and how to control them.

Some people are fervent about protecting whales or certain trees. They work with fervor, or with passion, to protect these living things. Sometimes people can speak fervently, or with great emotion. Patrick Henry, when he was working to make the United States a country independent from England, spoke these words with fervor: "Give me liberty, or give me death!"

Thelma Mitchell was born with a single limb, her left arm. Yet these physical handicaps did not stop Thelma's fervent desire to race in the New York City Marathon, a grueling run of 26.2 miles. With fervor, Thelma had built up her endurance and strength by wheeling her wheelchair farther and farther every day. On November 4, 1990, Thelma's fervent desire was met. It took her eight hours and 15 minutes, but she crossed the finish line. Is there anything about which you are fervent?

momentous

Wait a moment! How many times have you heard that phrase spoken? A moment is an instant, and *momentous* has the word *moment* within it. Ironically, when something is momentous, it is not momentary or only there for an instant. Momentous things are great and big. When something is momentous, it is important and has consequences that go beyond the moment. Something momentous is not petty.

Momentous things are so important that they catch everyone's attention. When our forefathers signed the Declaration of Independence and the United States became a new country, it was a momentous occasion. It was an important occasion that made our country into what it is today.

The day you were born was momentous—it was very important, and it changed the world. We have birthday parties to celebrate the momentous occasion of your birth.

Ment or *mem* mean "mind" or "memory" in Latin, and so if something is momentous, it is in our minds for a long time.

When a volcano erupts, is it momentous? Was man's accomplishment of walking on the moon momentous? Can you think of some momentous events in your life or in the world?

calligraphy

Can you figure out what *calligraphy* is from this rhyme:

> *With calligraphy did she write,*
> *Beautiful letters that were a sight.*
> *Perfectly formed and gorgeous to see—*
> *Unfortunately, such beautiful writing is not for me!*

Calligraphy is beautiful, elegant penmanship or writing. Picture the fancy lettering and words one finds on wedding invitations or how names are often printed on award certificates.

Kalli was the Greek word for beauty, and *graph* means "writing" or "picture," so *calligraphy* is beautiful picture writing. What is fun about the *kalli* root is that we can also hear it in *calisthenics*, those exercises we do to make our bodies beautiful!

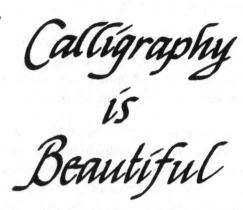

Before there were printing presses (invented in the 15th century by Gutenburg), people were hired to copy books by hand, carefully writing down every word! Think of how long it would take to write every word in your reading book! Not only did these people have to write down every word, but they had to write the words in beautiful calligraphy.

Why do you think your text books are not printed in fancy and ornate calligraphy?

mammoth

You are mammoth compared to an ant, but when you compare yourself to a blue whale, it is the blue whale that is mammoth, not you! What could *mammoth* mean?

Mammoth means big, huge, and enormous. Something that is mammoth is colossal; it is gigantic and of great size. You may also know the word *mammoth* from the animal known, in fact, as the mammoth. The mammoth, now extinct, was an early type of elephant that had lots of body hair and two long tusks which curved upward. It would be a mammoth problem if one found a mammoth is one's bathtub!

When one typically thinks of seeds, one thinks of little tiny things. But the giant fan palm found wild in the Seychelles (islands in the Indian Ocean) has a seed that weighs up to 44 pounds! Just one seed! That seed is mammoth!

The plant with the most mammoth leaves are again found on an island in the Indian Ocean. The mammoth leaves of the raffia plant are on the Mascarene Islands, and they measure up to 65½' in length. How would you like to have to rake those up every fall?

Would you go on a roller coaster ride with the name "Mammoth Drop"?

decorum

Do you chew with your mouth open? Do you lean way back in your chair? When one acts with decorum, in a decorous manner, one acts with polite and proper behavior. If you behave with decorum, you do not chew with your mouth open or lean way back in your chair.

In many societies, if one burps at the dinner table it is very rude. It is not decorous or proper behavior; it is not behaving with decorum. In some societies though, burping after a meal signals that one is full and well fed. It is not considered a breach of decorum.

When one walks down the halls at school or in a hospital, one should walk with decorum, with order. If one yells and shouts while racing down the halls, one would not be walking decorously. He or she would not be walking with decorum.

Because different countries and different societies have different forms of decorum, our government hires people to help make sure that our representatives behave with proper decorum so that no one is insulted.

Dinner is being served—what would the person behaving with decorum do with his or her napkin?

proficient

When one is proficient at something, one does really well at it. Proficient swimmers are skillful swimmers. They can swim across the pool and go into deep water. Proficient swimmers excel at swimming.

Babies can walk fairly early, but they are not proficient walkers when they first start out. They wobble all over the place, and they fall down easily. In just a few years, though, they are proficient at walking and go on to becoming proficient at riding a bike, skipping rope, and doing jumping jacks.

If something is efficient, it can be done without waste, and if one is proficient at something, one can do it efficiently and well.

Contrast how long it takes a human baby to become proficient at walking to baby zebras, animals who are proficient at walking just minutes after birth. What would happen to a baby zebra if it was not proficient at walking right away?

Is there something you are learning to be proficient at right now: singing, playing a musical instrument, running, reading, cooking, sewing?

slothful

Slothful is a great word! Think of the sloth, a mammal that lives in trees in South America. It moves very slowly. As a matter of fact, the sloth is so slow that it only moves an average of six to eight feet per minute on the ground. Try moving that slowly yourself some time. In a tree, the sloth speeds up to a whopping 15' per minute. Yet what can one expect from an animal that spends up to 80 per cent of its time sleeping or dozing?

If one is *slothful*, one is lazy and slow. One does not pick up after oneself, does not try, and puts out no effort at all. If one is slothful about school work, one does not bother to check spelling, erase mistakes, or ever remember to turn it in. One is slothful about his or her homework. The funny thing about the word *slothful* is that most people think that it came into being because of the animal. But the word *slothful* has been around for centuries. In the 12th century, the word *slou* was used to mean slow; the word slothful was recorded as early as 1390. When explorers first saw this slow-moving animal in South America that did not even stand when it fell from a tree, they called it a sloth because they thought it was slothful. Here is a conundrum: Is a sloth really slothful, or is it just behaving in its natural and proper way?

zealous

Can you get a feel for what the word *zealous* means from this rhyme:

> *Zealous Zeke had lots of zeal*
>
> *For the animal known as a seal.*
>
> *He had ardor, fervor, passion,*
>
> *For seals kept alive, not worn for fashion.*

Zeke was zealous about seals. When someone is *zealous*, they have lots of fervor about something. If someone has zeal for something, he or she is passionate and has great feelings. Zealous people have arduous feelings. Zealous people are eager and ardent in their pursuit of what it is they desire.

A zealous fan is one who loves his team more than anything. He or she knows everything there is to know about the team and attends every game. They are zealots when it comes to their team!

For years it was thought that dinosaurs were not good parents. They would lay their eggs and then go away. They would even eat their own babies later if they could! Now scientists are finding evidence that goes against this idea. Scientists now think that many dinosaurs were zealous parents, staying by the nest and protecting the eggs. When the babies hatched, they protected their babies zealously from other dinosaurs.

Do you have a teacher who is zealous about vocabulary?

toy

Every average child knows the meaning of the word *toy*. A toy is an object with which one plays; all of you probably have a favorite one. But what does *toy* mean in this sentence: "The cat toyed with the mouse." And in this sentence: "He toyed with the idea that one day he would be a teacher."

When a cat toys with a mouse, the cat is playing with the mouse, treating it as if it were a toy. The cat was probably letting the mouse get a little bit away and then pouncing on it and bringing it back. When the boy toyed with the idea that one day he would be a teacher, he played with the idea, thinking about becoming a teacher and wondering whether or not he would enjoy it.

When people toy with something, they are amusing themselves with it as if it were a toy. They are dealing with it lightly, without seriousness. They are flirting with it. When people says, "Don't toy with me," they mean that they do not want to be treated lightly. They want to be treated seriously.

Would one be wise to toy with a snapping turtle? What type of person would toy with another person?

competent

If one is competent, one is able and capable of doing something. Are you competent at peeling an apple? Are you able to peel an apple without any trouble? Are you as competent as Kathy Wafler, who created a 172'4" strip of unbroken peel from a single apple? This strange act of competence took 11 hours and 30 minutes.

Dr. Harold Williams is competent in a completely different area—speaking different languages. Dr. Williams can speak 58 languages fluently.

Are you a competent cook? Are you able to cook without problems? Could you competently cook what Bedouin chefs prepare for wedding feasts? That would be cooked eggs that are stuffed into fish, that are stuffed into chickens, that are stuffed into a roasted sheep's carcass, that is then stuffed into an entire camel. Do you feel competent that you would not burn this dish?

Look at the word *competition*. Do you see how closely it resembles *competent*? We have competitions to see who is the most competent or able to do something.

When people drink, they are not competent drivers. Their reflexes slow, and they do not react well or use good judgment. They become *incompetent* (*in* means "not"), and they should not be driving.

How long did it take for you to become competent on a bike? on ice skates?

estrange

From its sound, *estrange* may seem to be completely new, but when this word is broken down, it becomes familiar and makes perfect sense. How many of you can see the root *strange* in *estrange*? What does it mean to be strange? When something is strange, it is not normal; it is outside of what it usual. It is not part of the group any longer. A house with black curtains is strange, as is a person who will only wear red polka dots.

The "e" in front of *strange* in the word *estrange* is a prefix that we have seen before in words like *exit* or *emit*. The "e" means out or from. So if one is estranged, one is out of or becomes strange to the group. One is alienated and now apart from familiar surroundings or friends. One now feels disliked by those who once gave love or affection.

People may become estranged from each other after they fight or disagree about something. They become like strangers to each other because there isn't affection between them anymore. During the Civil War many families became estranged as one youth fought for the North and the other youth fought for the South.

It has often been said that during adolescence, children become estranged from their parents, and then later, after the children reach adulthood, they become closer again. Do you think that this is true? How do you keep from becoming estranged from your friends?

flaunt

If one wins a medal, should one *flaunt* it? Should one flaunt good grades? Should one flaunt a new bike?

If one flaunted one's medal, one would be waving it showily. He or she would be open and rude about flashing it about. Flaunting a medal would be having it where everyone had to notice it. If one flaunted good grades, he or she would be showing off about his or her grades. They would be sure to wave his or her scores in the air where everyone could see them. If one flaunted a new bike, he or she would be sure to ride it where everyone could see it.

Flaunting one's possessions or talents is not a friendly thing to do. It is wonderful to win medals, get excellent grades, and be given new possessions, but one should not take what is good for him or her and try to make others small. One should not show off. One should not be obnoxious about pointing out what he or she has or has earned.

When many male birds look for mates, they flaunt their feathers. They show off their bright colors to get the female bird's attention.

To attract tourists, some cities flaunt their attractions in tourists guides—famous parks, amusement rides, and unique museums. What could your city flaunt?

dissect

How do people learn about the unseen side of objects? How do people learn how things work? Students and scientists *dissect,* or cut things apart, to see what is going on. Through dissection, doctors learn how we work in order to help heal us and keep us healthy. *Sect* means "to cut," and we can see this root in *dissect.* We can also see *sect* in *bisect. Bi* means "two," and so when something is bisected, it is cut in two. A section of an orange is a piece of the orange, a piece that has been separated and cut out. A sector is a part of a whole. Computer grids are often divided into sectors, and each sector represents a certain area. When people call 911, people responsible for the sector from which the call originated respond to that call.

It is not just animals that are dissected. Difficult problems can be dissected, that is, cut or divided into little parts so that the big answer can be found. Can you dissect this problem and find the answer:

> *There was a terrible accident. Cars were totaled, and a father and a son were both rushed to the hospital where they both needed immediate surgery. The surgeon for the child raced into the O.R., scrubbed and ready to go. Yet as the boy was wheeled in and the sheet lifted so that the surgeon could begin cutting, the surgeon put down the knife and said, "I cannot operate on this boy. He is my son." How could this be?*

You can figure out that answer by dissecting the problem, breaking it into parts and analyzing it. First, there must be a parent/child relationship between the surgeon and the boy. The father was in the accident along with the son, so the one left is the mother. The surgeon, therefore, is the boy's mother.

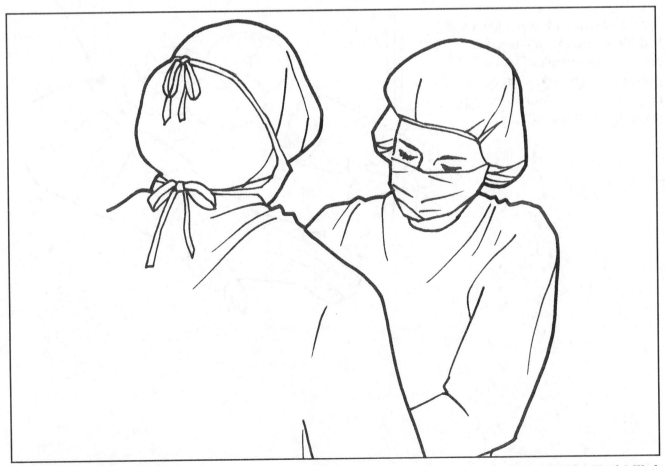

fracture

An earthquake hits, yet the new tall buildings do not fracture or break because they are built to earthquake code. These new buildings bend and sway. They do not break or fracture like buildings that are not built to code.

Fracture means "break." Children often suffer fractures when they fall off of monkey bars. There used to be many more head fractures in children but now that people are wearing bike helmets, there are less fractures and head injuries.

Fract means "to break," and we can see this *fract* root in the word *infraction*. An infraction is a breaking of a rule. In several states, children who ride their bikes without helmets are making an infraction of the rules. It is an infraction because it breaks the rules. *Fract* also shows up in *refracted*. Refracted light is light that is broken up. Think of how a pencil looks if you put it in a glass of water.

Our medical community has classified fractures into two types: simple and compound. Simple fractures do not involve broken skin, and compound fractures are fractures where the bone breaks through the skin.

Sometimes communities can become fractured if they do not all agree on something. Perhaps half of a city supports the building of an airport while the other half does not. The city has become fractured over this issue. Families, too, can become fractured over events. Hopefully, through talk and negotiation, such fractures can heal.

Have you ever dropped a glass and had it fracture into a thousand pieces? How many of you could package an egg so that when dropped off a one story building it would not fracture?

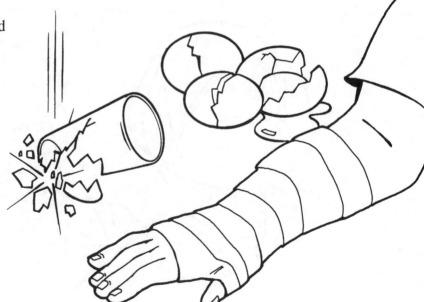

philanthropist

Which of these two people is the philanthropist: the person who speaks at an inner city junior high and promises to pay for college for every student who graduates high school, or the person who buys a baseball team and then raises ticket prices by 20 dollars a game?

Phil means "love," and we see it in *bibliophile* (lover of books), *anglophile* (lover of all things English), *Philadelphia* (city of brotherly love), and *philharmonic* (the love of music or harmony). *Anthro* means "man," and we see it in *anthropology* (the study of man) and *misanthrope* (a hater of man).

Putting *phil* and *anthro* together, we have *philanthropist*, and so we have a lover of mankind. A philanthropist does good and kind things for mankind. A philanthropist practices philanthropy.

There are many philanthropistic organizations. Can you name a few? Which club do you think would get the most members: one with the name The Misanthropical Society or the one with the name The Philanthopical Society? How do you think the members of each club would get along with one another?

Do you think that hermits are more likely to be misanthropes—haters of man—or philanthropes—lovers of man?

Can you think of something philanthropic that someone you know has done? Have you ever done anything philanthropic?

monstrosity

When one hears the word *monstrosity*, what usually comes to mind is *monster*. *Monstrosity* and *monster* are related, and since *monster* is already known, *monstrosity* should be easy to learn. A monstrosity is a freak, something that is abnormal. Two-headed kittens or calves with three eyes are monstrosities that did not develop normally.

Monstrous things can also be of great or terrifying size or complexity. Godzilla was a fictional monstrosity, a colossal lizard that destroyed everything in its path. Then there was a real monstrosity, a pumpkin grown in Canada in 1993 that weighed 836 pounds. Would you have enjoyed the monstrous task of turning that pumpkin into a jack-o'-lantern? Many children do not like to eat carrots. Can you imagine being given the monstrosity of a 6'10½" carrot grown in Great Britain in 1991 to eat?

Certain mazes or puzzles can be monstrosities, so difficult to solve that only a few people can solve them. See if solving this traditional riddle is a monstrosity:

> *As I was going to St. Ives, I met a man with seven wives.*
> *Every wife had seven sacks, every sack had seven cats, and every cat had seven kits.*
> *Kits, cats, sacks, and wives, how many were going to St. Ives?*

> Answer: One!

kindred

If one has a kindred friend, one's friend is of a like kind. Can you hear and see the root *kind* in *kindred*? Perhaps you are kindred souls or kindred friends because you both know what it is like to be lonely or you both enjoy the same activities. Perhaps you have had some of the same experiences or you think alike in the way in which you approach the world.

Can you also see and hear the word *kin* which is in both *kind*, meaning of the same type, and in *kindred*, meaning of a similar nature or related? One's kin are those to whom one is related.

Imagine being born a sextuplet (one of seven siblings all born at the same time), and you married someone who was also a sextuplet, as did each of your other siblings. Then you all had seven children! Imagine the number of uncles, aunts, and cousins your children would each have! What a large number of kin there would be to show up for Thanksgiving! Do you think you could remember the birthdays of all of your kin?

Many people join clubs to be with people who have kindred or similar interests. For example, the Sons of the Desert are loyal fans of old time Laurel and Hardy movies. Can you think of other clubs of kindred spirits?

vendor

Listen to this rhyme and think about the word *vendor*:

> *Belinda was a fruit vendor*
> *Selling peaches and mangos tender.*
> *But few people bought her plain fruit,*
> *And so she searched for a product to suit.*
> *Belinda then decided to bake*
> *Her delicious fruit into a cake.*
> *Belinda began to vend her wares,*
> *And people bought her cake from everywhere.*

If one does not already have a sense of the word *vendor* as someone who sells, one need only to think of *vending* machines. Vending machines are everywhere, selling colas, ice creams, candy bars, and stamps. There are even some vending machines that sell perfume, soap, and pencils or paper! *Vend*, then, means to sell. A vendor is one who sells. There are street vendors, selling their wares from carts or on tables they have set up along the street, and there are much bigger vendors who sell their wares in large malls. If any of you ever had a lemonade stand, you have experience vending. You were a vendor.

Many people believe that vending machines should not be allowed on school grounds because they do not vend healthy food choices. Do you agree?

cryptic

Many animals have cryptic markings. Animal markings are cryptic when they conceal or help the animal to hide. A zebra's stripes help hide or conceal them in a special way. A zebra is too big to hide the way we do in hide-and-go-seek, but it can hide in a large group. A lion comes to look for one zebra to chase, but with all the cryptic black and white stripes everywhere, the lion cannot tell where one animals starts and the other ends. The zebra is safe in the group because the lion cannot single it out.

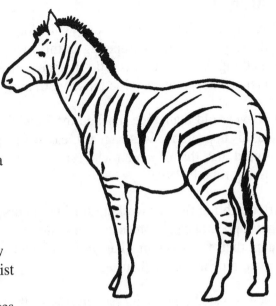

When things are *cryptic*, they are secret or unrecognizable. Cryptic messages are coded messages, messages that are concealed or hidden. A cryptologist studies codes and how to break them or create them. A cryptographer is a specialist in cryptography, the making and breaking of codes. The cryptographer may encrypt or put into code certain messages.

During World War II, the United States used a code that could not be broken by German spies. This code was the Native American Navajo language! The Navajo's language was too cryptic for our enemies; it could not be broken.

Can you find the answer to these cryptic riddles?

> Others use it more that you, but it is yours and yours alone. (Answer: your name)
>
> I can be felt but I cannot be touched. What am I? (Answer: the wind)

sophomore

Most of you may know that a sophomore is someone in his or her second year of high school or college (the class order is freshman, sophomore, junior, and senior), but how many of you knew that the part of the word *sophomore* came from a Greek word meaning foolish?

Moros means "foolish." But before you tease any sophomores you know, you must also realize that *sophos,* seen in the beginning of the word *sophomore,* is the Greek word for "wise." Sophisticated people are supposed to be wise in the ways of culture. Sophisticated machines are complex machines that can do many complicated things. Cars and computers are sophisticated machines. The practice of medicine has become very sophisticated, with fancy tests and medicines. Philosophers are scholars or thinkers, people who love wisdom. How did these two very different words get put together to create our word *sophomore*? Perhaps one has to be a sophisticated philosopher to figure it out! Some say that it is because with just a little bit of wisdom, some people don't know enough to know that they don't know enough! With just a little bit of knowledge, one can still be quite foolish. One is *sophomoric.* Sophomoric people are those who think that they know a lot, but they are poorly informed and immature.

Do you really think sophomores are sophomoric?

haggard

The Hawaii Triathlon is a race in which one swims 2.4 miles, cycles 112 miles, and then runs 26 miles and 385 yards. After competing in this race, one's appearance would be quite haggard. When something is haggard, it is wild in appearance. When one is haggard, one is gaunt, or having a thin and emaciated appearance. One looks worn and tired.

A 73-year-old man once finished the Hawaii Triathlon in 26 hours and 20 minutes. At the end of the race, his appearance was haggard, careworn, and drawn. Do you think his appearance was more haggard than that of a man who ran the marathon in eight hours, seven minutes, and 45 seconds, the winning time in 1993?

After fighting fires or working for long hours out in the fields, many people are tired and exhausted. Their appearance becomes haggard, and they need to stop and rest. When people do not get enough sleep, their faces become haggard, taking on a thin and tight appearance. They look careworn and drawn, pinched and exhausted.

There is a sled dog racing race in Alaska that takes place every year on the Iditarod Trail, a 1,049 mile journey from Anchorage to Nome. People spend years raising and training their sled dogs. The dogs have to work as a unit, and the person who races them must know each individual dog as well as they know themselves. Who do you think would look more haggard and exhausted at the end of the race, the person or the dogs?

Now that you know what *haggard* means, and how one looks if he or she has a haggard appearance, what do you think a hag is? A hag is a frightening old woman. Do you think a hag looks haggard?

flourish

When plants or animals flourish, they grow and develop well. When one's garden is flourishing, vegetables abound: corn, beans, peas, potatoes, pumpkins, tomatoes, and squash. Corn and soybeans flourish in the Midwest. What crops flourish in your state?

Businesses can flourish, too. Businesses can do well; they can make a profit and not lose money. Perhaps they have cheaper prices, and so they can sell more or perhaps they have a new or better product that people want and are willing to pay more for. Many fast food restaurants have flourished; one can find them not only in every state but also in other countries around the world!

Fluo is the Latin root meaning "to flow," and when something flourishes, it is as if it is flowing with life and strength, getting bigger and stronger, thriving and developing. The word *fluent* comes from the *fluo* root, and when one is fluent, one is able to speak clearly. The words flow freely. If one was bilingual, in how many languages would one be fluent? And note that a flute is an instrument where the air flows through it.

What do you need to flourish at school?

din

Listen to the following rhyme to see if you can figure out the meaning of the word *din*. Also, think about whether or not the character in this poem would make a good firefighter.

> *Screaming, yelling, crashing, banging!*
> *Horrendous, horrible, terrible clanging!*
> *Despite this cacophonous, ear-splitting din,*
> *Oblivious Jacob always slept in.*

A *din* is a loud, continous noise, a cacophony of harsh and discordant sounds. There is a racket or din in the school cafeteria when it is filled with hundreds of students. There are voices all raised up in different conversations, the noise of chairs scraping on the floor as students sit and stand, the clatter of silverware knocking against each other and falling to the ground, and trays clanging together—all at the same time. The noise is loud and continuous. It is a din.

In many factories there is a constant din of machinery, the noise from the machines being loud and constant. People who guide airplanes to their landing places must wear earphones to protect their ears from the constant din.

What did you decide about Jacob being a firefighter? At first thought, the answer would be that Jacob would make a terrible firefighter. If Jacob could sleep through a din, how could he ever be awakened to respond to a fire? Many people train themselves to sleep through anything (think of all the activity that goes in a firehouse) but can immediately wake up to a particular sound. Jacob may actually be an excellent candidate for a firefighter if he can sleep through the din, responding only to the alarm call.

Many parents can sleep through the din of traffic outside or the din of the television set, and they do not seem to be bothered at all by the noise. Yet when their child makes a sound, they wake up immediately. Somehow their brain filters out the din and focuses on what is important.

Have you ever created a din on New Year's Eve, banging pots and pans together to welcome in the New Year?

prologue

Listen to these words, given to you without context:

"She is in the hospital. She ate ice cream. Oh, her head came off! Well, good-bye head. Let's have some more ice cream."

What do you think about these words? You probably have no idea about the who, what, or where behind them. One would be clueless as to what was really going on. Yet if one had read a *prologue*, or a short introduction, explaining that one was going to hear the comments of a 3-year-old who was playing with an old doll, one would immediately understand this strange talk. A prologue, or introductory statement, would have cleared things up.

Prologues appear in many books. Often a prologue is just a paragraph or two explaining when the story takes place or who exactly someone is before the main chapters start. A prologue is the preface or introduction in a book or a speech given at the beginning of a play. A prologue is the introductory event.

Logue means "speaking" or "speech," and we find this root in many words dealing with speech. A dialogue is a speech between two people (*di* means "away," and so the speech goes from one away to the other), and a monologue is a speech by one person (*mono* means "one.") An epilogue is the ending speech or the ending part of book that concludes what happens. A eulogy is a speech of praise, and often when there is a memorial service, the eulogy helps us remember all the good and wonderful things a person did.

At a school program, would you rather say the prologue or the epilogue? Why?

radiant

If someone was described to you as having a radiant personality, would you expect that person to be warm and bright or unfeeling and dull? Before you answer this question, think back to the book *Charlotte's Web*. Charlotte was a spider who saved the life of Wilbur the pig. Charlotte wove in her web the word "radiant" to describe Wilbur. Charlotte would not write anything negative about Wilbur, and thus *radiant* must be a positive word. Someone who is radiant is warm and bright.

Radiant has to do with light. Radiant light is bright, shiny, blazing, and brilliant. The sun's light is radiant; it shines brightly from light radiating from the burning gases.

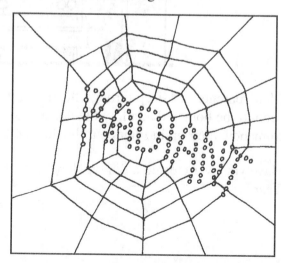

Radiant can also be used to suggest warmth. Smiles can be radiant in that they make one feel warm and liked. When things appear radiant, they do not seem dark and dim. A radiant child is one who is loving and happy, glowing with life and energy.

If one lived in the far north, how could one keep one's self feeling radiant and cheerful in the winter when the sun did not shine?

hypochondriac

A person listens to a doctor on the radio describing a strange new strain of a common disease, such as the flu. As the person listens to the symptoms—teary eyes, swollen glands, sinus headache—the person begins to wonder about the slightly itchy throat he or she had that morning. Soon the person is feeling his or her throat, trying to detect swollen glands. Soon, the person is at the doctor's office describing symptoms, but the doctor finds there is no actual disease.

Such a person is a hypochondriac. A hypochondriac is someone who worries all the time about his or her health. A hypochondriac worries incessantly about the way he or she feels. He or she is sure there are heart problems, stomach problems—any problems. Yet even though the hypochondriac goes from doctor to doctor, the doctors can never find anything wrong with him or her.

Hypos is the Greek root meaning "under" (think of a hypodermic needle that goes under the skin) and *chondros* is the Greek root for breastbone. Seems like a strange combination of roots to be making up the word *hypochondriac* with its meaning of "one who is always concerned with one's health and convinced that he or she is ill." It makes sense, however, when you learn that the Greeks believed that right underneath the breastbone was the abdomen, and that all worries about one's health came from the abdomen.

It is so common for beginning medical students to become hypochondriacs, believing they have all the symptoms of the strange new diseases they are learning about, that the teachers actually warn them about being hypochondriacal ahead of time.

When a hypochondriac really becomes ill, do you think sometimes it is like the boy who called wolf—that the doctor will not take him seriously because of the number of times the hypochondriac complained and said he felt things when there was really nothing wrong with him?

punctual

Can you guess what the word *punctual* means from this rhyme?

> *Punctual Kate was never late,*
> *Arriving promptly on the dot.*
> *"Don't make others feel second rate," said Kate.*
> *"Being fashionably late is a lot of rot."*

Kate arrived promptly on the dot. Kate was punctual, showing up exactly at the time for which she was invited. *Punctus* is the Latin root for point, and when one is *punctual*, one is right on the point of time.

Punctus is also found in *puncture*, when a hole is made in something with a sharp point. When one punctuates or uses punctuation in a sentence, one is putting in various points (periods, commas, etc.) so that the sentence can be understood correctly. If one is *punctilious*, one is exact and always following the proper points of behavior or rules.

What would you do if you were supposed to go with a friend to a movie which started at a specific time and he or she was not punctual?

initiative

What are your initials? Your initials are the beginning letters of your name. Your initials are at the start of your name.

When one has or shows initiative (note the similarity between *initial* and *initiative*) one starts or takes the first step toward doing something. If one has initiative, one has the energy to start something. When one acts on one's own initiative, one is acting on his or her own, without someone telling one to do it.

Nothing ever rots on Mount Everest. It is too cold, and so any garbage left there is there forever unless it is carried down. With all the expeditions up to the mountain, the amount of garbage was incredible—cans, bottles, broken equipment, and even human waste. On their own initiative, some climbers organized an expedition where the purpose was to clean up the mountain. No one told them they had to do it. They did it on their own initiative, starting the clean up because it was the right thing to do.

Perhaps you think your school needs something. You could wait forever, or with initiative, you could start working for it. Do you think inventions are more likely thought up by people who have initiative or by those who wait for someone to tell them what to do? The wheelbarrow is said to have been invented in 230 AD in China. Do you think the inventor showed initiative? Was initiative shown in 1489 when Johann Widman invented the + and - signs in mathematics? Is there a time when you showed initiative?

pusillanimous

Say the word *pusillanimous* several times and listen to it carefully. In all honesty, would you like to be called *pusillanimous*? Does *pusillanimous* sound like a favorable, positive word? Can you imagine stopping to eat a picnic in the beautiful countryside, the hills a deep green, a clear clean brook bubbling along at one's feet, the sun warm and pleasant on one's face, and turning to someone and saying, "How pusillanimous!"?

Now listen to this rhyme and see if you can figure out what *pusillanimous* means and whether or not you would like to be considered pusillanimous.

> *Always fearful and creating a fuss,*
> *Timid Tim was pusillanimous.*
> *Cowardly and always afraid,*
> *Pusillanimous Tim was never brave.*

If one is pusillanimous, one is cowardly. Pusillanimous people are marked by contemptible timidity; they are so timid that they will never do anything on their own unless it is for their own good. They are mean and petty.

The Latin word *pusillus* means "tiny," and pusillanimous people are tiny and small when it comes to their minds and their souls. The Latin root *animus*, meaning "mind," is found in *pusillanimous* and in lots of other words you may know. Think of *animal*, *animated* (brought to life, like cartoons), *inanimate* (not living, like a rock), and *unanimous* (all of one mind; *unus* is Latin for "one"!).

It is normal to be nervous or afraid of many things, such as when one first learns how to swim or ride a bike. One is not being pusillanimous in those situations; one just has normal nervousness. One is pusillanimous if one is afraid of doing things to the point where one wants everything given to him or her. They are so fearful that they are not willing to try anything new. A pusillanimous person would turn in a friend, even if he or she was not sure if the friend really did what he or she was accused of, just so that he or she would not be blamed. I am sure that none of you are pusillanimous.

Can you think of any pusillanimous villains in the cartoons or movies that you watch?

alibi

You are accused of stealing all the cookies from the cookie jar! Despite the fact that you have cookie crumbs on your lips, you have an unshakable alibi. You have an excuse or a reason why it could not be you. Your alibi was that you were at your friend's house and ate there. When your friend is questioned, not only does he support your alibi, but his mother says that she was there with you, too, and your alibi becomes even stronger. Your alibi, your explanation for why you could not have done it, is unbreakable.

Where did we get this word? *Alibi* is the Latin word for elsewhere, and back in the 18th century, at a criminal trial, the verdict was stated as, "We the jury, find that the accused was alibi." That is, the jury found that the person accused was elsewhere. He could not be guilty because he had an alibi; he was not there.

Over the years, *alibi* was used so often in the courts that it spread to everyday speech. Now, an alibi is one's story or excuse or explanation as to why one could not have done something.

Would the prosecuting or defending lawyer like the accused to have an unshakable alibi?

surcease

Stop! Halt! Cease! Desist! Do you think you know enough synonyms for "stop"? Perhaps not, because you are about to add one more to your list. *Surcease* means to stop, to cease, to end, and to discontinue what one is doing. Do you hear the root *cease* in *surcease*?

Charles Osborne of Indiana hiccuped every 1.5 seconds for 69 years and 5 months. He led a reasonably normal life, but no matter what he did, his hiccups would not surcease. He could not stop his hiccups.

One may think that we have a crazy language with too many words, but all of our words make our language rich and full of meaning. We can paint pictures with our words, and our stories become textured and filled with details that express exactly how we feel. Imagine learning English as a second language—one would have to learn all the ways to say *stop*, including *surcease*!

Donna Griffiths once sneezed without surceasing for 978 days. It is estimated that she sneezed over one million times in the first 365 days alone. Think of all the tissues she must have used!

foremost

If someone asked you, "Michael Jordan was the world's foremost basketball player—agree or disagree?", it would be important for you to know what the word *foremost* meant before you answered.

Foremost means that something is first or most important. When something is foremost, it is the best, the finest, superior in every way. It is the most forward in its class.

Many of you may recognize the word *fore* in *foremost*. *Fore* means "at an earlier time period" or "at the beginning" (think of *before*). When golf players hit the ball, they yell, "Fore!" It is believed that this cry, used for over a century, came from the word *before*, and that golfers started using it when the harder golf ball came into use in 1878. Nice to be warned before the hard ball hits one's head! *Fore!*

Perhaps you hear a principal speaking, and he or she begins by saying, "First and foremost, one has to learn to read and write." By saying, "first and foremost," the principal is emphasizing how important it is to learn to read and write first.

Will your class have complete agreement on this next question: Who is the foremost actor of our time? How about the foremost baseball player? Foremost singer? Foremost band?

Knowing that *foremost* means that it is the first in time, place, or order, can you figure out what these words mean:

foreman:	*the first or chief man, like the head of a jury or a group of workers*
foresight:	*the ability to see ahead*
forecast:	*a prediction of what is going to happen next*
forefathers:	*our ancestors; our fathers who came before*
foremother:	*your female ancestors*
forefinger:	*the index finger, the finger that comes first*
foreleg:	*a front leg*
forelock:	*a lock of hair growing from the front of the head*

latter

Listen to this rhyming riddle and take a guess at whether the answer will be pears or apples.

> *A choice of pears, yellow, then apples, red,*
> *Arranged just so on a lettuce bed.*
> *Lucy thought and reached for the latter,*
> *Making the decision with little chatter.*
> *So without the former, but the latter,*
> *Pear or apple did she take from the platter?*

The latter is that which is at the end. Lucy took the latter, and it was the apples that came after the pears, so Lucy took an apple from the platter, having chosen the latter.

People often give preferences by stating, "I will take the former," or "I will take the latter." The latter choice is always that choice which is presented last.

Did any of you recognize the word *former* (when Lucy chose the latter instead of the former) as being related to *fore* or *before,* being at the front or at the beginning? The former is that which comes before. The latter is what comes after, or later.

For excellent school work, you can earn an award of five extra minutes of lunch every day for a week or 10 bonus points on any English paper. Will you chose the former or the latter?

throng

Throng. Throng. Isn't *throng* a funny-sounding word? A throng is a group, a crowd, a band, or a clique of people.

Throng is a word that we use when we are talking about a crowd that is moving toward a destination or that moves aimlessly. A circus may be attended by throngs of people. Great throngs of people jam into coliseums to see their favorite teams play. Have you ever gone to the movies and gotten caught in the throngs of people, all waiting to buy popcorn at the concession stand?

The president has bodyguards to keep back the throngs of people who want to touch him or talk to him. Movie stars and sports figures also sometimes travel with body guards. What do you think of having to travel in public in this fashion? Would you enjoy having throngs of people pushing at you?

Throng can be used both as a verb and a noun. Is *throng* a verb or noun in these sentences:

1. *Throngs came to see the giant pandas at the zoo.*

2. *People thronged to the giant pandas' enclosure when the bears awoke from their snooze.*

prominent

Listen to this rhyme and see if you can figure out what the word *prominent* means:

> *A prominent tail had Fargo the Cat,*
> *It stuck out incredibly far from its mat.*
> *Everyone had to carefully step 'round*
> *Fargo's prominent tail or risk tripping down.*

Fargo's tail stuck out. His tail was prominent. When something is prominent, it stands out or is conspicuous. A prominent tail would be a really noticeable tail. A prominent tail would be a tail that stands out from all other tails.

Pro means "forward," and something that is prominent is forward. Pinnochio had a prominent nose, and with each lie that Pinocchio told, the nose became even more and more prominent, pushing more forwardly out with every false word.

Someone can become prominent; this person can be said to have prominence. Such a person is noticed and is widely and popularly known. Our presidents are prominent figures. They are on the news, and their pictures are hung in every government building. We have prominent sports heroes, and we have prominent artists and musicians. Perhaps there is someone you really love or admire. You may place their picture in a prominent place, a place where there is no chance whatsoever of the picture ever being missed.

The Golden Gate Bridge in San Francisco is a prominent part of San Francisco's landscape. Have you ever been there? What would one consider a prominent feature of New York City? Chicago? What would you consider a prominent feature of where you live?

hasten

You have gone to visit a friend who is the proud owner of a 14' python. Halfway through the meal, your friend tells you that the python has been missing for about a week, but not to worry, for it will show up when it is hungry. Just then you feel something wrapping itself around your leg. Do you *hasten* your eating or do you continue at your relaxed pace?

When one hastens, one accelerates. One moves quickly, going to a fast rate of speed. If one moves with haste, one goes swiftly. A hasty decision is one that is made quickly and hurriedly. A hasty decision is made with great speed and without much thought.

Perhaps one hastily dresses in the morning, hastening so as not to be late. One arrives at school and realizes that perhaps he or she were too hasty, for he or she is wearing his or her shirt inside out. At this point, one should hasten to the restroom and turn the shirt right side out!

Have you ever done your homework with haste? How do your parents get you to hasten out of bed?

rebate

Try and figure out what the word *rebate* means from this rhyme:

> *Rita got some money back,*
> *And that's a monetary fact.*
> *She sent in box tops and a sales receipt—*
> *Got a whopping rebate of two dollars to keep.*
> *What Rita did not know*
> *Is that the item's price was two dollars more—*
> *So even with rebate, she was just as poor.*

A rebate is a return of a part of a payment. A rebate is when one gets something back. Have you ever seen advertisements where they say to you excitedly, "Get a thousand dollars cash back!" The thousand dollars cash back is a rebate; it is part of your payment paid back to you.

Rebates aren't always given because of an advertising ploy. Sometimes rebates are given because something was wrong with what you bought, and the store gives you some cash back to make up for what was wrong.

We often hear about tax rebates. We all pay taxes for our roads, health care, schools, and government. Sometimes more taxes are collected than what we should have had taken from our paychecks. When this happens, most people want rebates. They want their cash back. Others feel that the collected taxes should be used for special expenses or to improve schools. Tax rebates are a hotly debated item in an election year.

Re is a prefix that means "again" or "back" (think of *return* or *renew*), and with a rebate, one is getting something back. One is diminishing or blunting the price or whatever it is that one is doing.

Rebate has an interesting origin. The word *rebate* comes from a sporting term! Can you guess from what sport *rebate* originated? Falconry! *Rebate* meant "to bring back a bating hawk," and what this meant is that the hawk had left its perch without being told that it could do so, and one had to *rebate*, get the hawk back.

Even though falconers wear thick heavy gloves, would any of you be interested in rebating a hawk? How would you do it?

124

orchestrate

When you hear *orchestrate*, you most likely think the word *orchestra*. Orchestras are violins, cellos, violas, bassoons, flutes, pianos, oboes, clarinets, and percussion all playing together while a conductor waves a baton up and down. Yet the vocabulary word this week is not *orchestra*, it is *orchestrate*. How many of you think there is a connection?

An orchestra is a collection of musicians playing a variety of instruments, but they are all playing together. They are organized and being directed by someone who is telling them when to play and when to get louder and softer. Keep this playing together and being organized in mind when one goes to the word *orchestrate*.

When something is orchestrated, it is organized. It is arranged or combined so that a maximum effect is achieved. If someone orchestrates the school day, one decides when school will start, when buses will unload, how long classes will be, when lunch is eaten, what schedule of classes one takes, and when the day will end. The person who orchestrates the school day has to direct bus drivers, work with teachers, deal with school boards, make sure custodians have time to do their work, follow state guidelines, and more.

Many fast food restaurants are carefully orchestrated. People working behind the counter are supposed to get the customer's meal items in a certain order. It has been orchestrated for speed.

Surgeons have orchestrated procedures before surgery. They make sure that everything is sterile and that all the equipment is ready and working before they start.

Who orchestrates the dishwashing and house cleaning in your house?

commendable

Who should be commended? Which one is commendable, the person who returns the wallet he or she found or the person who says, "Anyone foolish enough to lose a wallet shouldn't have a wallet, and therefore I have the right to keep it"?

If something is commendable, it is praiseworthy. Heroes are commended for their brave actions. If one returns a purse that he or she has found, one should be commended because one has done a commendable act. One has done what is right.

Com is a prefix meaning "intensive," and *mendare* comes from Latin and means "to entrust." When something is commendable, it inspires in us a great feeling of trust. A commendable person is someone who has a great deal of credibility. Can you think of some commendable students? community leaders?

dogged

One hears the word *dogged*, and one immediately thinks of the common domestic animal, the dog. Yet if one is dogged or behaving doggedly, it does not mean that one is running around on all fours, snapping at the teacher's legs, or barking at the principal who happens to be walking down the hall. Try to figure out what dogged actually means by listening to this ditty:

> *Louis was a dogged cat*
> *Who stubbornly chased the ugly rat.*
> *Louis the cat would not give up.*
> *And in the end on the rat did sup.*

Dogged means that one is stubbornly determined. A dogged person is tenacious and does not give up trying. If one behaves doggedly or with doggedness, one keeps on trying and does not give up.

Many people believed that Helen Keller, a woman who became blind and deaf at an early age, would never talk. But Helen Keller proved them wrong. With dogged effort and the help of her tutor, Anne Sullivan, Helen Keller was able to say, "I am not dumb now."

In the early 1900s, the Wright brothers doggedly worked on creating flying machines. They went from gliders to a powered plane in 1906 that could stay aloft for an hour.

How many people in your class will doggedly think about these two patterns until they have figured out how the patterns were created?

3, 3, 5, 4, 4, 3, 5, 5, 4, 3

(**Hint:** The next numbers are 6, 6, 8, 8. Pay attention to how the numbers are spelled. The **number one** has three letters.

31, 28, 31, 30, 31, 30, 31

(**Hint:** The next numbers are 31, 30, 31, 30. There are only twelve numbers in this series, and then it repeats, over and over. Think of how many days there are in each month.)

ingrate

Goldilocks was an *ingrate*. She was a rude child who entered a house to which she had not been invited. She ate the bears' food, broke their furniture, and slept in a bed that was not hers. When the bears returned, Goldilocks did not even bother to thank her hosts. Ingrate that she was, she ran home as fast as she could.

An ingrate is someone who is not grateful or thankful. An ingrate is not appreciative of what they have or what is done for them. *In* is the Latin prefix meaning "not," and when the *in* is placed in front of *grate,* it means that the person is not grateful. A grateful person is one who is thankful and appreciative.

We should be grateful for our libraries. It used to be that only the very rich could afford books. With our library system, anyone can borrow books and read them. We are thankful that books are available to everyone.

If something is gratifying, it is pleasing to one; one appreciates it. People's thirst cannot be gratified by salt water, since drinking salt water makes them thirstier. It is fresh water that gratifies or satisfies (pleases) one's thirst. When people express gratitude, they are showing that they are appreciative or are thankful. An ingrate does not express gratitude. A tip, the extra money we leave for a waiter or waitress, is a gratuity. It demonstrates that we are pleased with the food and service and are thankful for it. In some countries or restaurants, the gratuity is automatically added on to your bill. Do you agree with this practice, or even tipping?

Would an ingrate say, "Don't bite the hand that feeds you?"

milk

All of you know what milk is—the nutritious liquid that comes from mother mammals. Most of the milk we drink comes from dairy cows. In some places though, the primary sources of milk are goats. What does the farmer do to get the milk from the cow? The farmer milks the cow. He extracts or draws the milk out of the cow.

The word *milk* can be used as a verb in a different context. Sometimes if a person tries to get everything he or she can out of an experience, we say that person is trying to milk the experience for all it's worth. An example might be when a person goes to a tiny carnival with a big admission price. The person goes on every ride, plays every game, and eats every kind of junk food offered, even if these things aren't very good. The person is milking the experience.

The oldest child often thinks that the youngest child milks the experience of being the baby for all it is worth. In this way, the youngest child makes a profit out of or gets as much out of being the youngest as he or she can. Perhaps he or she does not have to do as many chores. Would you agree?

When famous people cut to the front of the line and expect to be allowed into an event first, are they milking their stardom?

temperate

Would a temperate child be more likely to throw a temper tantrum than a child who is not temperate?

Would you adjust your vote if you knew that the climate in Garapan on Saipan in the Mariana Islands in the Pacific Ocean, is considered to be one of the world's most temperate? For over nine years, the temperature only ranged from 67.3° F to 88.5° F. Would these islanders ever be in need of fur coats or air conditioners?

When something or someone is *temperate*, it is moderate and mild. There are no extremes when one is talking about something that is temperate. A temperate child, then, would be more likely to keep his temper and would be less likely to have a temper tantrum.

However, if one is temperamental or behaving temperamentally, one's mood or character is constantly changing. One's mental state is going up and down when one is temperamental. (It is almost as if one's body temperature goes up and down, fluctuating wildly every day!)

Temperamental eaters may eat pizza one day, and the very next day they may say that they hate pizza. Are you temperamental when it comes to Brussel sprouts or are you clear on how you feel about them?

Is it nice to be temperamental with one's friends? Is it fair to be kind and generous with them one day and the next ignore them?

mimic

The monarch butterfly reportedly tastes terrible. Its distinctive coloration warns predators of its bad taste. The viceroy butterfly, on the other hand, is *edible*, meaning it can be eaten. Yet it *mimics,* or looks very much like the monarch butterfly. The viceroy butterfly *mimics* the monarch butterfly so that it will not be eaten.

When something is mimicking or practicing mimicry, one is imitating closely or copying. There are some harmless snakes that mimic rattlesnakes. They shake their tails in dry leaves, mimicking the rattling sound of rattlesnakes. Would you stop to find out if the rattle was being mimicked or would you depart hurriedly?

Mimicking people's mannerisms can be funny, but it can also be cruel. One should not make fun of others by mimicking them. Are mimes, silent actors that use movement, gestures, and expression to express their themselves, good mimics? Can you all mimic a monkey? a slug? a nervous mouse?

quest

Can you get a feel for the word *quest* from this rhyme:

> *There is a river of gold,*
> *And a fountain of youth, I'm told.*
> *A worthwhile quest*
> *To seek out west.*

A quest is a search. When people go on quests, they are searching out answers. Throughout history, many people have gone on quests to look for rivers, gold, and yes, even fountains of youth. Why do you think explorers who quested after the fountain of youth have never completed such quests? Could it be because there is no such thing as a river of gold or a fountain of youth?

Searching for a fountain of youth may be a silly quest, but there are many good quests. How about the quest to cure cancer or other diseases?

Many people think that the quest to find life forms on other planets is a waste of time. Other people think that this search for extra terrestrial life is a worthwhile quest. What do you think?

Note the similarity between *question* and *quest*. A question asks something. If we question something, we are searching for and seeking out an answer to it. We are making sure that we have no doubts about the matter.

A *query* is a question. When we query something, we are questioning it. We are searching out the truth. Some scientists had lots of queries about hair. Their queries were answered when they studied hair and found out that hair grows at the rate of one half an inch a month, that hair grows slower at night than it does during the day, and that between 10 and 11 AM, the speed of growth is at its greatest.

If one requests something, one is asking for something. *Re* is a prefix that means "again" or "back" (think of *redo* or *remake*), and so if one requests something, one is asking for something back. One wants the answer or the result of the quest brought back to them. It has been said that the pursuit of knowledge is a life-long quest. Do you agree?

genealogy

What was your great great grandfather's name? Did your grandmother have 13 brothers? Are you related to the Queen of England?

Genealogy is the study of one's lineage or one's pedigrees. Genealogists study one's ancestors. Through birth records, old documents, oral and written histories, and even searching through graveyards and looking at the inscriptions on tombstones, genealogists try to fill in family trees. Genealogists attempt to find out whose relatives are whose and where people came from. To study something is seen in the affix *ology*. *Genos* is Greek for "race," and the letters *gen* are used in many words to refer to birth, race, or kind. Genealogy is the study of one's family heritage.

How many of you can curl your tongues? Curling your tongue is a talent that cannot be taught. It is genetic. It is carried through our genes, the part of our chromosomes where our hereditary from one generation is transferred to the next.

Can any of you generate, or give birth to, ideas as to why a tongue that can curl is superior to one that cannot?

A generation is a group of people born at the same time. Your parents are one generation, you and your siblings are another generation, and your children will be the next generation. How many living generations are there right now in your family?

salutary

How is sneezing connected to the word *salutary*? If one hears a person sneeze, what does one usually say? In Latin American countries, the typical response is *salud*. *Salud* means "health" in Spanish, and one wants one to remain in good health. Sneezing of often a sign of an impending cold, and *salud* is said in hopes that one will remain in good health.

Do you see most of the root *salud* in *salutary*? If something is salutary, it promotes good health or is beneficial. Before we had the antibiotics to cure tuberculosis, doctors used to send their patients to New Mexico and Arizona. The dry air there had a salutary effect.

Salutations are expressions of greeting and goodwill. Salutations have a salutary effect. Isn't it easier to feel good and happy and healthy when people greet you warmly? It would be hard to feel good if no one smiled at you or didn't bother to greet you.

Back to sneezing! When one sneezes, germs are spread throughout the air. This does not have a salutary effect on the people around you! Proper etiquette says one should not sneeze at the dinner table. If one feels a sneeze coming on, one should excuse himself or herself. Sometimes sneezing cannot be helped, but no matter what happens, one should never blow one's nose at the table. There is nothing salutary about noseblowing at the dinner table!

Does getting enough sleep have a salutary effect on one's mood?

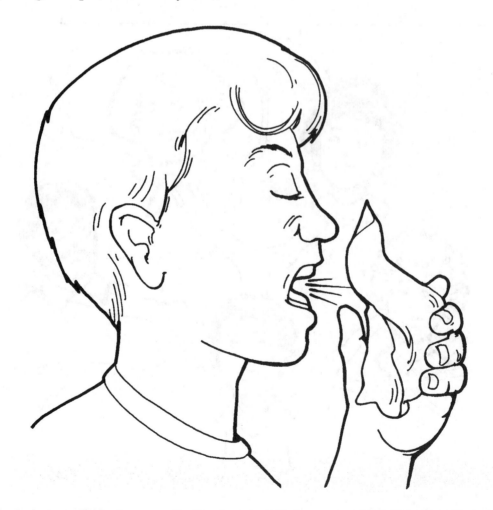

Glossary

acute sharp, pointed; mentally keen; less than 90 degrees

affluent rich; wealth; having a lot of

agile able to move quickly and easily

alacrity promptness and speediness in response, cheerful readiness

alibi an excuse or reason why one could not have been somewhere or done something

alleviate to lighten, to make easier to do or to be endured

alma mater the school where one has attended or graduated from

altruistic unselfish, giving

amass to gather into a great mass, accumulate, collect

ambidextrous able to use both hands equally well

amble to walk aimlessly

amicable friendly, peaceable

antiquated out of date, old fashioned

apathetic not caring, without feeling, lack of interest

ardent to have great feeling and passion for; fiery and hot

arduous very difficult, hard to do

articulate to speak distinctly and clearly; intelligible

assimilate to become similar; to absorb and become part of

audacious daring, bold; insolent

audible can be heard

avid wanting to the point of greed

benevolent kind, giving, charitable

bibliophile lover of books

boisterous wild and full of energy; noisy and rowdy

cacophony harsh or unpleasant sounds

calligraphy beautiful and elegant handwriting

chronic all the time, repeatedly

circumvent to make a circle around; stopping something from happening ahead of time or by being clever

claustrophobia fear of closed in places

colossal really big, enormous

commendable praiseworthy

Glossary (cont.)

competent able, enough ability to do well

conundrum a riddle, an unsolved puzzle

cosmopolitan from many parts of the world; universal; free from prejudice and at home anywhere in the world

credible believable, trustworthy

cryptic secret, in code, serving to conceal or puzzle

cull to select from a group, choose

decorum with proper behavior and manners, with orderliness

defenestration throwing of a person or thing out of a window

dehydrated to lose water

desist to stop, cease

din a loud continued noise, confused and discordant sounds

discordant harsh and unpleasant sounds; conflict, opposition

disgruntled not happy or content, ill-humored

dissect to separate into pieces; to analyze

doff to take off or lift up; to remove from one's body or self

dogged stubbornly not giving up, tenacious

egregious conspicuously bad or outlandish

elite a superior group, those who are the top or best in a particular group

embolden to make bold, to inspire with courage

emit to send out, discharge

endurance able to be strong and survive; capable of withstanding hardship; having great stamina

equivocate to go back and forth, to not be able to make a decision

erudite learned; having great knowledge about something

estrange to alienate; to remove from one's usual environment or friends

extricate to free from whatever is holding or tangling one up; to get out of a messy situation

extrovert an outgoing person

feasible capable or able to be carried out, can be done

ferret European polecat often used for hunting; to drive out of a hiding place; to find and bring to light by searching

fervent very hot or glowing; having great burning feelings or passion towards something

Glossary *(cont.)*

figuratively the opposite of literally; symbolicly; using words to describe something which creates a particular image or feeling. For example, "She is a tiger on the soccer field." Tiger is symbolic, creating an image of her behavior on the field—wild, ferocious, and dangerous.

flaunt to wave or flutter showily; to show off in a way no one can miss

fledgling a young bird with newly developed feathers; also an immature and inexperienced person

flourish to grow well, to thrive and prosper

foremost in the first place, the most important; first in a series, order, or rank

fracture break, rupture or tear

fraternity brotherliness, brotherhood; a social (for fun) or professional (for work) club of males

frivolous of little importance; not serious

frugal sparing, economizing, careful of what is spent or used

garrulous chattering, talkative, wordy

genealogy the study of one's lineage (family tree) or pedigree

glutton one who eats too much; can't get enough

gregarious social, likes to be in a group

gullible easily tricked or deceived, willing to believe anything

haggard wild in appearance, gaunt and emaciated, tired and careworn, exhausted

hasten to accelerate, to move or act quickly and hurriedly

herpetology the study of reptiles and amphibians

hodgepodge a mixed up collection, a jumble, an assortment

hypochondriac someone who thinks only of health and worries constantly that he or she is quite ill

impeccable perfect, without fault

inanimate not living, not animated

incessant without stopping, continuing without interruptions

inclement cold, wet, harsh

incognito with identity hidden or a different name, in disguise

ingrate an ungrateful person, someone who is not thankful or appreciative

initiative an introductory or beginning step, starting something on one's own without

waiting to be told

innocuous harmless

insatiable can't be satisfied, can't be sated

insipid dull, tasteless, lacking flavor

insomnia the inability to fall asleep

intrepid fearless, brave

interminable never ending, going on forever

itinerary a route of a proposed journey or the outline of one; a schedule of what you plan to do

irk to annoy, to bother, to irritate

kindred of a similar nature or character, related

kudos awards, honors; compliments and praises

latter the most recently said, or that which was presented at the end (so it was heard or presented the most recently); the second or last in a group of things being referred to

lethargic without energy, slow moving

levity without seriousness, with lightness, with frivolity

literal exactly as it was spoken

ludicrous ridiculous, silly

magnanimous big hearted, giving, generous, noble

malicious bad, without good intentions

mammoth really big, gigantic, huge

marshal a high official (as in a town marshal); a putting in proper order or position; a bringing together and ordering; ushering

mellifluous sweetly flowing

milk to draw or extract profit from, to take advantage of

mimic to imitate closely; to make fun of or ridicule by imitation

mollify to soften, to make feel better; to reduce in intensity

momentous important and consequential

monotone sounds all in the same tone or voice

monstrosity a freak, something unnatural; something of great and terrifying size or complexity

myriad a very big number, so big one is not sure exactly how many!

novel a made-up book, fiction; something new

Glossary (cont.)

obdurate stubborn

oblivious unaware, not noticing, not paying attention to

omnivorous eating everything, devouring all kinds

optimist a person who always puts or see things in the best possible way

orchestrate to arrange or combine so as to achieve maximum effect

oscillate to swing back and forth like a pendulum ; to keep changing one's position

pacific calm and peaceful

parsimonious stingy, very sparing in what one uses

paternalistic treating in a fatherly manner

pedestrian ordinary, commonplace

pell-mell in mixed up confusion or disorder; confused haste

perturbed upset

pessimist a person who always puts or sees things in the worst possible way

petrified turned into stone, made rigid and still with fear and awe

petty small, of little importance; acting with narrowness and meanness

philanthropist a lover of mankind; one who does good deeds that help people

placid peaceful, calm, undisturbed

plethora a lot, an abundance

pod a seed vessel; a group of whales, seals, or sea lions; compartment under the wings of an aircraft.

potent powerful, with great strength; effective

prodigy a wonder; a highly talented child

proficient skilled and good at something, able to do it well

prolific fruitful and fertile; producing a lot

prologue an introduction or beginning of a book, a speech given as a forward, an introductory event

prominent standing out, readily noticeable and conspicuous, widely and popularly known, leading

punctual always arriving or doing things at the correct time

pusillanimous cowardly, contemptibly timid

quadruped having four feet

Glossary *(cont.)*

quest a search; a journey to find something

radiant glowing, shining brightly; warm and brilliant

rebate a return of a part of a payment, money back

retrospect to refer back; to reflect back on

rupture break or burst by violence; a tearing apart

sage a wise person; an herb

salutary promoting good health, beneficial

scintillating to sparkle, to be brilliant

serpentine winding and turning; sly and crafty

Sisyphean relating to or as difficult as the punishment of Sisyphus

slothful incredibly lazy

sophomore a second year student in high school or college

steadfast firmly fixed in place; not changing what one believes; loyal

stoic not affected by or showing passion or feeling; showing no response to pain or distress

stymie to block, to frustrate

subaqueous under water

superfluous extra, a surplus

surcease to stop, to come to an end, to discontinue

taciturn usually silent, not inclined to talk

tantalize to tease or torment; to be desirable but just beyond reach

tarry to be slow in leaving; to be tardy; to delay; to stay at one place

taxidermist one who prepares, stuffs, and mounts animal skins

tedious tiresome because of length or dullness, boring

temperate moderate and mild, not extreme or excessive

tenacious to hold on, to stick to something without giving up

throng a great crowd, a large number; to pack into, to crowd into

toil to work long and hard; to do tiring and exhausting work

torpid no energy; having lost motion or power of exertion

toy to play with; to treat lightly and without seriousness

Glossary *(cont.)*

transgress to go beyond set limits; to violate or break a law or command

trudge to walk or march steadily with great effort or work

turbulent causing violence or great disturbance; marked by agitation and great movement

upbraid criticize, scold severely

urbane courteous, polite, polished, suave

valid having strength and force; convincing and sound

vendor one that vends or sells, a seller

verbatim word for word

versatile turning with ease from one thing or position to another; able to do many different things

vex to irritate, annoy, or trouble; to puzzle

vilify to say evil and mean things about someone or something

vivacious full of life, animated

vociferous with great noise, shouting, loud and insistent, boisterous

voracious greedy in eating, ravenous; can't be satisfied

wane grow smaller gradually, to lose strength

wax to increase in size, number, strength, length or volume

whimsical acting on a sudden desire, without planning ahead

witty being clever in a fun and silly way with words

zealous full of zeal, eagerly, with lots of passion and desire

zenith directly overhead; at its highest point

Bibliography

Gilman, E. Ward, Senior Editor. *The Merriam-Webster Thesaurus.* Pocket Books, 1978.

Hendrickson, Robert. *Encyclopedia of Word and Phrase Origins.* Facts on File, Inc., 1997.

Lansing, Alfred. *Endurance: Shackleton's Incredible Voyage.* Carroll and Graf Publishers, Inc., 1959.

Leokum, Arkady. *Tell Me Why #2.* Grosset & Dunlop, 1986.

Lewis, Norman. *Word Power Made Easy.* Pocket Books, 1978.

Matthews, Peter, Editor. *The Guinness Book of Records 1995.* Bantam Books, 1995.

Peters, Max and Jerome Shostak. *Barron's How to Prepare for High School Entrance Examinations SSAT ISEE Seventh Edition.* Barron's Educational Series, Inc., 1988.

Rappaport, Doreen. *Living Dangerously: American Women Who Risked Their Lives for Adventure.* HarperCollins Publishers, 1991.

Robinson, Jacqueline, Dennis Robinson, and Eve Steinberg. *ARCO High School Entrance Examinations.* Macmillan, 1996.

Shortz, Will. *Best Brain Teassers.* B and P Publishing Company, Inc., 1991.

Stonaker, Frances Benson. *Famous Mathematicians.* J.B. Lippencot Company, 1966.

Thomas, Lydia Austill, Executive Editor. *New Reading Skill Builder 4, Part 2.* Reader's Digest Services, Inc., 1967.

Wexo, John Bonnett. *Zoobooks: Sharks.* Zoobooks, Vol. 5, Number 12. Wildlife Education, Ltd., 1988.

Woolf, Henry Bosley, Editor in Chief. *Webster's New Collegiate Dictionary.* G. & C. Merriam Company, 1977.

Woolf, Henry Bosley, Editor in Chief. *The Merriam-Webster Dictionary.* Pocket Books, 1974.

Index

Index (cont.)

Index *(cont.)*

Index *(cont.)*